Frommer's™

Cuba
day BY day™

1st Edition

by Claire Boobbyer

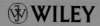
WILEY

A John Wiley and Sons, Ltd, Publication

Contents

The Savvy Traveler 157

UK Publisher: Sally Smith
Executive Project Editor: Daniel Mersey
Commissioning Editor: Mark Henshall
Development Editor: Don Strachan
Content Editor: Erica Peters
Cartographer: Tim Lohnes
Photo Research: Jill Emeny

Wiley also publishes its books in a variety of electronic formats. Some
content that appears in print may not be available in electronic books.

British Library Cataloguing in Publication Data
A catalogue record for this book is available from the British Library

ISBN: 978-0-470-72161-2

Typeset by Wiley Indianapolis Composition Services
Printed and bound in China by RR Donnelley

5 4 3 2 1

A Note from the Editorial Director

Organizing your time. That's what this guide is all about.

Other guides give you long lists of things to see and do and then expect you to fit the pieces together. The Day by Day guides are different. These guides tell you the best of everything, and then they show you how to see it *in the smartest, most time-efficient way*. Our authors have designed detailed itineraries organized by time, neighborhood, or special interest. And each tour comes with a bulleted map that takes you from stop to stop.

Hoping to cruise the streets of the Malecón in a classic car or sip Mojitos in Old Havana? How about finding a tiny beach cove hideaway in Guardalavaca or a carnival in Santiago de Cuba? Planning a drive through Cuba discovering the tropical island's sugar cane, palm trees, rum, music, and revolution? Whatever your interest or schedule, the Day by Days give you the smartest routes to follow. Not only do we take you to the top attractions, hotels, and restaurants, but we also help you access those special moments that locals get to experience—those "finds" that turn tourists into travelers.

The Day by Days are also your top choice if you're looking for one complete guide for all your travel needs. The best hotels and restaurants for every budget, the greatest shopping values, the wildest nightlife—it's all here.

Why should you trust our judgment? Because our authors personally visit each place they write about. They're an independent lot who say what they think and would never include places they wouldn't recommend to their best friends. They're also open to suggestions from readers. If you'd like to contact them, please send your comments our way at feedback@frommers.com, and we'll pass them on.

Enjoy your Day by Day guide—the most helpful travel companion you can buy. And have the trip of a lifetime.

Warm regards,

Kelly Regan

Kelly Regan, Editorial Director
Frommer's Travel Guides

About the Author

Claire Boobbyer is a travel writer, photographer, and editor who fell in love with Latin America more than 10 years ago after several backpacking trips around the region. She moved to Spain to learn Spanish and, after a stint of working with wildlife in the Peruvian Amazon, headed north to Central America. She first went to Cuba in 1998 to spend a newly reinstated Christmas Day holiday in Havana and has been returning ever since. She is the author of several other guidebooks on the region and her photographic work has appeared in various guidebooks and alongside her travel articles. She is also the current author of *Frommer's Cuba*. She is available for consultation about Cuba at claireboobbyer@btinternet.com.

Acknowledgements

Claire Boobbyer would like to thank the editors and team at Frommer's and the many Cubans across the country who gave her assistance on the ground, and always the warmest welcome.

An Additional Note

Please be advised that travel information is subject to change at any time—and this is especially true of prices. We therefore suggest that you write or call ahead for confirmation when making your travel plans. The authors, editors, and publisher cannot be held responsible for the experiences of readers while traveling. Your safety is important to us, however, so we encourage you to stay alert and be aware of your surroundings.

Star Ratings, Icons & Abbreviations

Every hotel, restaurant, and attraction listing in this guide has been ranked for quality, value, service, amenities, and special features using a **star-rating system.** Hotels, restaurants, attractions, shopping, and nightlife are rated on a scale of zero stars (recommended) to three stars (exceptional). In addition to the star-rating system, we also use a **kids icon** to point out the best bets for families. Within each tour, we recommend cafes, bars, or restaurants where you can take a break. Each of these stops appears in a shaded box marked with a coffee-cup-shaped bullet ☕.

The following **abbreviations** are used for credit cards:

AE	American Express	**DISC**	Discover	**V**	Visa
DC	Diners Club	**MC**	MasterCard		

Frommers.com

Now that you have this guidebook to help you plan a great trip, visit our website at **www.frommers.com** for additional travel information on more than 4,000 destinations. We update features regularly to give you instant access to the most current trip-planning information available. At Frommers. com, you'll find scoops on the best airfares, lodging rates, and car rental bargains. You can even book your travel online through our reliable travel booking partners.

A Note on Prices

In the "Take a Break" and "Best Bets" sections of this book, we have used a system of dollar signs to show a range of costs for 1 night in a hotel (the price of a double-occupancy room) or the cost of an entree at a restaurant. Use the following table to decipher the dollar signs:

Cost	Hotels	Restaurants
$	under $100	under $10
$$	$100–$200	$10–$20
$$$	$200–$300	$20–$30
$$$$	$300–$400	$30–$40
$$$$$	over $400	over $40

An Invitation to the Reader

In researching this book, we discovered many wonderful places—hotels, restaurants, shops, and more. We're sure you'll find others. Please tell us about them, so we can share the information with your fellow travelers in upcoming editions. If you were disappointed with a recommendation, we'd love to know that, too. Please write to:

Frommer's Cuba Day by Day, 1st Edition
Wiley Publishing, Inc. • 111 River St. • Hoboken, NJ 07030-5774

20 Favorite **Moments**

20 Favorite **Moments**

1 Havana Streets
2 Communist Propaganda in Havana
3 Vedado
4 Old Havana
5 Malecón
6 Viñales
7 Playa Las Estrellas
8 Rural Cuba
9 Bay of Pigs
10 Remedios & Gibara
11 Trinidad
12 Playa Pilar
13 Southern Coastal Road
14 Casa de las Tradiciones
15 Santiago de Cuba Carnival
16 Ballet Folklórico Cutumba
17 Guardalavaca
18 Casa de la Trova
19 Baracoa
20 Malecón

A heady mix of beaches, music, rum, and Revolution unfurls across the tropical island of Cuba. Conquered by the Spaniards and reinvigorated by African and Haitian slaves, its cultural blend is evident in rhythm and tunes, religion, architecture, and in its people. Combined with a natural beauty of white sands, turquoise seas, palms, mountains, and flourishing flora and fauna, a trip to this beguiling land will surely see you heading back for more. Here are 20 of my own favorite experiences.

Cruising in a classic car.

1 Cruising the streets and Malecón in a classic car. Feast your eyes on the chrome wings and other glinting accessories of Havana's 1950s American cars, and then hire one to glide through the crumbling streets. *See p 164.*

2 Glimpsing the communist propaganda in Havana. I love wandering Havana to see life as it's lived on the tumbledown streets. Turn a corner here and there and you'll be surprised to see billboards and communist slogans extolling the virtues of the Revolution painted across walls, doors, and windows.

3 Sundowners and sunset in Vedado. As the sun sets in the west, the Malecón and Old Havana are bathed in the late afternoon light. For music and a de rigueur mojito, step onto the terrace of the Hotel Nacional. For the best aerial views of Vedado and the Malecón, climb the Focsa tower and admire the 360° panorama of the city while sipping a cocktail in La Torre. *See p 41 and p 110.*

4 Mojitos in Old Havana. Eschew the pricey La Bodeguita del Medio and El Floridita and opt for a table in the Plaza de la Catedral. The cathedral's baroque lines undulate all day but this drinking spot is cooler in the later hours. *See p 27.*

Drinking mojitos in Plaza de la Catedral.

5 Braving the Malecón during a storm surge. When the sea gets wild, the Malecón and its seaside buildings get battered by furious waves that lurch over the ocean wall; the results of salt erosion can be seen on the buildings and pavements. It's an exciting time to be on the Malecón, but watch out for your camera.

6 Walking the Viñales countryside. Viñales' valley floor is crisscrossed with tobacco fields and other crops, and views are interrupted by the soaring *mogote* (limestone stacks covered in vegetation). A day in the valley will see you wander past ploughing oxen, farmers on horseback, and the sweet, pastel-colored huts of farmers, as well as others used for tobacco-leaf drying. This is rural Cuba at its best, witnessing the timeless relationship between humans and the earth. At sundown, admire the valley views from the pool or top terrace of the confectionery-pink Hotel Los Jazmines. *See p 152 and p 155.*

7 Searching for starfish. Playa Las Estrellas is a remote point on Cayo Jutías. Although you can take a boat there, turn your day into a Robinson-Crusoe adventure instead, and walk past sculpted driftwood and virginal sands to the cay's point where you can spot gigantic orange starfish. Remember to take water and a hat, because there's no shade. *See p 52.*

8 Driving through rural Cuba. A road trip through Cuba's countryside is a unique experience: there's barely a road sign and just a handful of other vehicles. The tall Cuban Royal Palm, lengthy stalks of sugar cane, farmers with hats on horseback, and working oxen provide the backdrop, along with dozens of large communist billboards daubed

Southern coastal road.

with slogans and pictures of the heroes of the 1959 Revolution. *See Chapter 5.*

9 Touring the Bay of Pigs. This historic site, off the regular tourist trail, saw the failed US-backed invasion to overthrow the new government of Fidel Castro in 1961. This whole chilling stage-set sits in an area of outstanding beauty. The deep blue color of the water awash with plates of aquamarine blue is inviting for snorkelers and divers and the area is rich in birdlife, easily spotted on one of the many trails. *See p 78.*

10 Diverting from the tourist route. Cuba has a concentration of Spanish colonial cities with preserved historic cores. Escape the crowds by heading to the coast to see the untouristy towns of Remedios and Gibara. Sit in the plaza and drink in the local cafés to blend in, undisturbed by hustlers. *See p 132 and p 81*.

⓫ An afternoon stroll in Trinidad. The late afternoon light in Cuba is perfect for photographers. I like to escape its small colonial core and wander into the cobbled back streets to watch and snap the end-of-day activities. *See p 146*.

⓬ The most beautiful beach in Cuba? Not particularly easy to get to, the creamy, undisturbed sands at Playa Pilar on Cayo Guillermo roll out at this island's tip. The vibrant, turquoise shallow sea laps at the shore. Walk the length of the beach early in the morning before the day-trippers arrive. *See p 74*.

⓭ Wild driving on the southern coastal road. The weather-beaten coastal road between Pilón and Santiago de Cuba is remote and dramatic. It takes you past a canvas of lashing waves and cliffs that drop vertically onto the ocean road, which itself lies just yards from the sea. At times the road rollercoasters

and the panoramic scenery unfolds below. After hurricanes and bad storms, parts of the road and bridges are lost, making for some hair-raising driving; this is not a trip for the faint hearted but it's the best drive in Cuba. *See p 83*.

⓮ A night in the Casa de las Tradiciones. Tucked into a street in the El Tivolí district of Santiago de Cuba is this small music venue where live bands perform to locals and the few tourists who step out of the city center. It's authentic, and the only place in town where Cubans might outnumber the tourists. The mojitos go down a treat too. *See p 145*.

⓯ Pitching up for carnival. There's no more exciting time to be in Cuba than during July's Santiago de Cuba carnival. It's a riot of conga processions, parades, musical interludes, and drinking beer from giant vats. You can catch up on sleep during a break in the festivities on 26th July, which marks the 1953 Moncada attack. *See p 160*.

Baracoa's setting from on high.

16 Watching a folkloric dance group. Cuba's most talented group is Santiago's Ballet Folklórico Cutumba. The colorful and energetic Afro-Cuban dance and performance is mesmerizing. *See p 145.*

17 Beach hideaways. Around the northern coastal resort of Guardalavaca are tiny coves reached from some of the hotels. Most holidaymakers don't bother searching them out, and so if you do find them, it's likely to be just you, the beach, and that aquamarine sea. *See p 81.*

18 Humming the tunes at the Casa de la Trova. Baracoa's Casa de la Trova is one of the most authentic *trova* houses in the country. Cubans and tourists mix, take a twirl on the dance floor under the whirring ceiling fans, and sip mojitos into the balmy, tropical night. It's the perfect Cuban night out. *See p 145.*

19 Viewing Baracoa's setting from on high. Most people agree that Baracoa nestles in one of the most scenic spots in Cuba. To really take in the view, climb the hill to the Museo Arqueológico and check out the miradors. Spot the curvature of the Bahía de Miel surrounded by curtains of lush tropical vegetation. Down below, the jostling, higgledy-piggledy terracotta roofs of the town's buildings spread out towards the **Malecón**. *See p 114.*

20 Walking Havana's Malecón at sunset. At sundown, Havana's ocean road and the craggy rocks below are crowded with fishermen, dog walkers, children swimming offshore, women gossiping, and lovers smooching. Havana's so-called 'open-air living room' is the place to head to spend the last hours of daylight. *See p 13.* ●

Sunset walk along the Malecón, Havana.

1 **Strategies** for Seeing Cuba

Strategies for Seeing Cuba

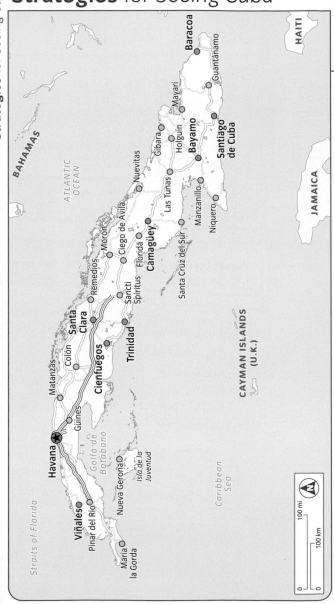

Cuba is a large island and although there's little traffic on the roads, some journeys will take longer than anticipated due to the serious lack of decent road signs. Even with a good road map, you'll almost certainly need to stop and ask directions. A good phrasebook, a pen, and paper may be useful if you don't speak Spanish. Here are some strategies to help you enrich your time and travels.

Rule #1: Weigh up the pros and cons of car rental

Cuba is served by an efficient tourist bus service, Víazul, which provides daily services linking key towns across the island. It's reasonably priced and comfortable, but take a sweater for night journeys due to the air-conditioning. To travel anywhere beyond these key points, you need to hire a car or rent a taxi. Hiring a car allows greater freedom and flexibility. Gas stations have increased in number and official parking lots are available for overnight parking. Travelers will need the Guía de Carreteras (a map guide), available to buy from Infotur (see p 105) in Havana. See p 165 for information about Cuban hitchhikers.

Rule #2: Allow for down time

Don't cram your days full of activities. Cuba is a tropical country and the heat can be intense, especially between 1pm and 3pm. Coupled with the fact that you may have unexpected bureaucracy to tackle, always have a Plan B. If you're on the road and thinking about a lunch break, it's better to pull over at the first roadside restaurant/gas station you see because it may be the only one for miles. These places aren't somewhere to linger; they're purely (limited) refreshment stops.

Rule #3: Time your visit right

Cuba's cultural calendar is positively bursting with possibilities. If you're a party animal, brave the suffocating heat of Santiago in July. If you're a movie fan, visit in December. For cigar aficionados, a festival takes place in February, when the tobacco fields are also in bloom. The coolest months are between December and March, and to escape a capitalist Christmas, come for a winter break; Christmas is low-key in Cuba. For more on the festival calendar, see p 159.

Rule #4: Decide whether to hotel-hop or stay in one place

Cuba is a large country but some of the region's most popular stops are relatively close to one another. By choosing a base for several days and exploring the surrounding area on day trips, you save time checking in and out of rooms. However, if you wish to explore from beach resorts such as Cayo Santa María, Cayo Coco, and Guardalavaca, you will need a car. Or it may be more relaxing to

Car rental.

Playa Guardalavaca.

book accompanied tours with the hotel's tour desk.

Rule #5: Take children into account

The displays of many of Cuba's museums don't engage young visitors, a problem not helped by a lack of English-language signage. Cuba's greatest appeal for children is its street life, nature, and beaches. You would do well to plan for variety on your vacation. Remember to stock up on bottled water wherever you go; children dehydrate faster than adults. Many *casa particular* (private rooms for rent) owners are very accommodating to travelers with children. ●

Know Where You're Going

Hard currency is desperately sought-after in Cuba, and hustlers, known as *jineteros,* are usually one step ahead of the game. *Jineteros* meet incoming buses with the names of tourists they've gleaned from friends inside the bus company. They then tell the visitors that a reservation at a specific *casa particular* (private rooms for rent) has been canceled or that they're taking them to that casa, when in fact they're heading to a different one altogether. If you trust your confirmed reservation at a casa, make sure you know the exact address and location, and distrust touts who direct you elsewhere. False name boards have even been attached to unlicensed *casas*. Some *jineteros* have arrived at casa doors with unsuspecting tourists, pulled out a false set of keys and announced 'Oh, the owner isn't here because the door's locked'. The *jinetero* then takes visitors to his or her friend's house and earns commission. Car drivers are also approached by pedestrians and bicycles 'offering help'. If you accept help to find your way to a casa or *paladar* (restaurant in a private home), a CUC$5 commission will be added to your bill.

The Best **Full-Day Tours**

Havana in a **Long Weekend**

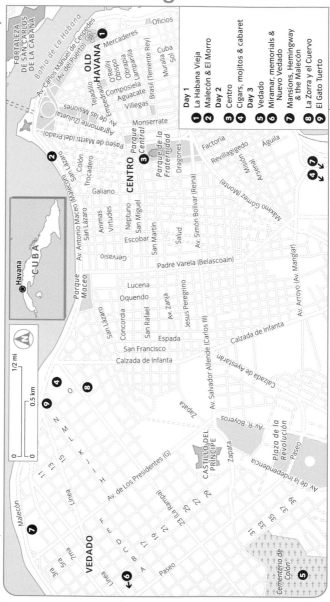

Havana is a fairly large city with many of its principal attractions spread out across three main districts. There are plenty of taxis to move between them and a new city tourist bus, Habana BusTour, and so it's easy to cover a lot in three days. You can expect to dip into everything this city is famous for, although you may need more than a long weekend to visit every important and exciting sight and take in the famous nightlife: attempting day-long sightseeing and night-long dancing and drinking is exhausting in the tropical heat. START: **Habana Vieja.**

Day One

❶ La Habana Vieja. Start the morning off in **La Habana Vieja** (p 98). Visit the Plaza de la Catedral, the cathedral, the Plaza de Armas and its second-hand book stall, Plaza Vieja, and Plaza de San Francisco. Be sure to tour the **Museo de la Ciudad** (p 91), on the Plaza de Armas and the **Castillo de la Real Fuerza** (p 91), and any other attractions that catch your attention. Have lunch at **La Bodeguita del Medio** (p 35).

Spend the afternoon wandering the streets, perhaps checking out the craft market close to the cathedral, parading up and down the main shopping street, Obispo, or just admiring the restored Spanish colonial architecture. There is so much architectural wealth and plenty of social activity in La Habana Vieja that you could be there for weeks just soaking up the atmosphere, sights, and street life.

❷ Malecón & El Morro. As the day cools down, take a stroll on the **Malecón** (p 94). Along the section nearest La Habana Vieja you will see men fishing off the rocks and families passing the time. Then head to the **Parque Histórico Morro y Cabaña** (p 95) in a taxi because it's open late. Stick around for the *cañonazo* (cannon-firing) ceremony (p 94) and a meal or, alternatively, after you watch the sun set on the Malecón, head for drinks in the Plaza Vieja at **La Taberna de Muralla** (p 106) and then dinner at one of the old city's attractive restaurants, preferably one with outdoor seating such as **El Portal** (p 105) or **La Dominica** (p 105).

Malecón & El Morro.

The baroque Gran Teatro, Centro.

Continue the evening by wandering up Calle Obispo and ducking in and out of the bars, the majority of which feature live music. If you're feeling flush, opt for a daiquiri at one of Hemingway's favorite watering holes, the Floridita (p 35), at the edge of the Old City.

Day Two
❸ **Centro.** Spend the day exploring the area around Parque Central, which includes **El Capitolio** (p 95), the **Museo Nacional de las Bellas Artes** (p 93), and the **Museo de la Revolución** (p 94). Admire the statue of José Martí, the art deco splendor of the **Bacardi building** (p 39), the classic facade of the **Hotel Inglaterra,** the baroque splendor of the

Cementerio de Colón, Vedado.

Gran Teatro, and the view from the rooftop pool of the **Hotel Saratoga** (p 100). Take lunch at **Los Nardos** (p 106) opposite the **Capitolio.**

❹ **Cigars, mojitos & cabaret.** Make a reservation in advance for the 2pm tour of the **Partagás cigar factory** (p 95). After visiting one or two of the other attractions in the area (see above), walk up the pedestrian boulevard **El Prado** and admire the contrasting architecture on both sides. Stop at **Hotel Sevilla** (p 100), made famous by Graham Greene in *Our Man in Havana*, for a drink. If you have the energy, you should be able to make the 20–30 minute walk to the **Hotel Nacional de Cuba** (p 41) along the **Malecón** (p 94) in time for a sunset mojito at their outdoor bar. In the evening, head to the **Tropicana** (p 110) for dinner and a show.

Day Three
❺ **Vedado.** Start the morning strolling among the tombs and mausoleums of **Cementerio de Colón** (p 97). From here, head over to the outdoor art exhibit that is the **Callejón de Hammel** (p 96). If your third day is a Sunday, arrive here early for the Sunday rumba sessions, which are frenetic, hot, and very busy. By now, you should have worked up enough of a sweat for a refreshing bowl of ice-cream at **Coppelia** (p 96). Admire the architectural icons close by: the **Universidad de La Habana, Hotel Habana Libre** (p 103), the **Yara Cinema,** and the **Hotel Nacional** (p 41). Wander La Rampa, as Cubans do, right down to

the sea. There's a small craft market here.

❻ Miramar, memorials & Nuevo Vedado. From Vedado, take a Coco Taxi to **Miramar** and the **Playa district.** Be sure to visit the **Maqueta de la Habana**, a rather impressive mock-up model of the entire city. Since you're out in this neck of the woods, have a late lunch at **La Cocina de Lilliam** (p 108). After lunch, head to the **José Martí Memorial** (p 97), and enjoy the panorama from the highest spot in Havana. Then, imagine the **Plaza de la Revolución** full to bursting during a political rally and admire the iconic image of Che Guevara cast in iron on the **Ministry of the Interior building** opposite the memorial.

❼ Mansions, Hemingway, & the Malecón. If there's time in the afternoon, return to the leafy streets of **Vedado** and admire the mansions including art deco (p 38) and art nouveau delights. If you're a Hemingway fan you may wish to book a tour that takes you to his farm on the outskirts of Havana and rushes you through his favorite drinking places afterwards. Late afternoon, take a pre-booked old American car for a glide down the *Malecón (p 94). There's no better way to view the coastal road, essentially Havana's open-air living room. Just before sunset is best as the light is beautiful.*

Musical evening. In the evening, take a late dinner at the gorgeously located **La Guarida** before ducking into **❽ La Zorra y el Cuervo** or **❾ El Gato Tuerto** in Vedado for some late night entertainment. One-off events are notoriously difficult to track down, but you can catch Buena Vista Social Club stars such as Omara Portuondo and the famous national ballet for very reasonable prices. Ask at your hotel desk for music events and at the Gran Teatro for the ballet. *See also 'Festivals', p 159.*

Travel Tip

For full details on touring Havana see p 88 in Chapter 6.

Image of Che on the Ministry of the Interior building, Plaza de la Revolución, Vedado.

Cuba **in One Week**

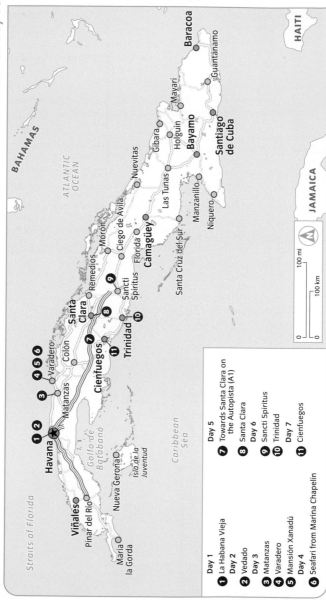

Seven days in Cuba allows you to spend time at the beach as well as take in the historic cities of Santa Clara and Trinidad, in addition to Havana. Varadero provides the perfect escape to swim and sunbathe. Cuba is a large island and so you'll need to arrange accommodation at all your stops. And be warned: estimating journey times by kilometers is fraught with difficulties, because Cuba's roads are often bad and road signage is virtually non-existent. So, always allow more time than you think. START: **Havana.**

Travel Tip

For hotels, restaurants, and detailed information on sights, see Chapter 5 for Varadero (p 71) and Cayo Santa Maria (p 73) and Chapter 6 for Havana (p 88), Santa Clara (p 136), and Trinidad (p 146).

Day One

1 La Habana Vieja. Spend your first day in La Habana Vieja and, in addition to the sights mentioned in **1** and **2** on p 13, squeeze in a horse carriage ride or a trip to the

Sábado de la Rumba, Vedado, Havana.

Sábado de la Rumba, a mesmerizing show of Afro-Cuban religious and secular music and dance at El Gran Palenque. *C/ 4 e/ Calzada and Av 5, Vedado on Saturdays at 3pm. For a full tour of Havana, see p 88 in Chapter 6.*

Day Two

2 Vedado. Take time over the highlights listed in **2** and some of those in **3** on p 91. Remember that the tropical heat in Cuba can be exhausting and you may not have time to fit everything in, and so be judicious in your choices.

Day Three

3 Matanzas. From La Habana Vieja, drive east under the tunel de la Bahía that separates El Morro from the old town. This good main road will take you 142km (88 miles) (2½ hours) along the coast to Varadero. You skirt the eastern beaches of Havana known as **Playas del Este.** Closer to Matanzas you pass the **Bacuanayagua Bridge** with its viewpoint across the countryside. (p 72). If the beach can wait, drive into **Matanzas,** 36km (22 miles) from the beginning of the hotel strip, to view its small collection of sights. *See p 128.*

4 Varadero. Cuba's largest beach resort has more than 17,000 hotel rooms spread along a 23-km (14-mile) peninsula. A thin line of fine white sand fronts a calm stretch of Caribbean Sea. The hotel accommodation is a mix of architectural horror and inviting plantation-style, low-key resorts. Pick wisely (p 75), and then spend the afternoon on the beach.

5 Mansión Xanadú. If you want to explore, go for a sunset drink on the terrace of **Mansión Xanadú.** After dinner at your hotel or in a restaurant in town, opt for a night at **the Casa de la Musica,** Av. Playa (📞 45/66-8210); the **Cabaret Continental,** Hotel Varadero Internacional (📞 45/66-7038); or the **Tropicana Matanzas,** Autopista a Varadero 4½km (3 miles) (📞 45/26-5555).

Day Four
6 Seafari from Marina Chapelín. Spend the day on or under the water. All the mid-range and top-end hotels offer watersports, and you'll be able to organize activities either with the hotel's nautical club or excursions desk. In the evening take a seafari, a sunset catamaran tour from **Marina Chapelín.** See p 23 and 71.

Hostal Florida Center.

Varadero beach, Matanzas province.

Day Five
7 Towards Santa Clara on the Autopista (A1). Leave Varadero early to drive to Santa Clara, a good half-day away. Return to Matanzas before heading east along the Autopista (A1), following the occasional signs. There are signs to the **Centro Histórico** on Santa Clara's huge ring road.

8 Santa Clara. Santa Clara is Che Guevara's city, and there are two important sights related to him to visit (p 138). If Spanish colonial interiors pique your interest visit the **Museo de Artes Decorativas** (p 137). In the early evening, head to **Parque Vidal,** the downtown heart and soul of Santa Clara, and then on to **Hostal Florida Center** (p 139) for dinner where you'll also be staying the night (p 139). After dinner, see if anything is happening at **Club Mejunje** (p 138). For more on Santa Clara see p 136.

Day Six
9 Sancti Spíritus. Head east out of Santa Clara on the Autopista in the

To and Around Varadero

If you decide not to rent a car until you reach Varadero, take the three-hour Víazul tourist bus (p 164) journey from Havana to Varadero at 8am, 10am, or noon. While in Varadero, take the VaraderoBeachTour bus (☎ 45/66-8992) that plies a loop from one end of Varadero to the other and offers an unlimited-journeys day pass for CUC$5. It has abandoned a timetable but there are plenty of stops along the peninsula and you won't have to wait too long. Alternatively, there are plenty of taxis, horse-drawn carriages, and Coco Taxis if you need to move quickly. The Víazul bus station is at Calle 36 and Autopista del Sur in the town end of the beach resort.

morning. If you're interested in colonial towns, stop for a short wander in untouristy **Sancti Spiritus,** set off the highway 83km (52 miles) from Santa Clara. From Sancti Spiritus, head 70km (43½ miles) south to **Trinidad,** past the former sugar center of **Valle de los Ingenios** (p 149).

⑩ Trinidad. After choosing your accommodation (p 150), spend the afternoon touring Trinidad's colonial-era landmarks, and then make a dinner reservation at **Paladar Estela** (p 151) or **Sol y Son**. After dinner, visit the **Casa de la Música** (p 109), or the excellent **Palenque** **de los Congos Reales**. *See p 151 in Chapter 6.*

Day Seven
⑪ Cienfuegos. Spend an hour in the morning shopping at the street markets before heading back to Havana. Or, if you prefer to see the city of **Cienfuegos** for an hour or so, leave Trinidad early via the 81km (50 miles) of coastal road to Cienfuegos. On leaving Cienfuegos, head north through **Palmira** to **Ranchuelo** for access to the Autopista back to Havana. Trinidad to Havana takes around five hours without stops.

Trinidad.

Cuba in Two Weeks

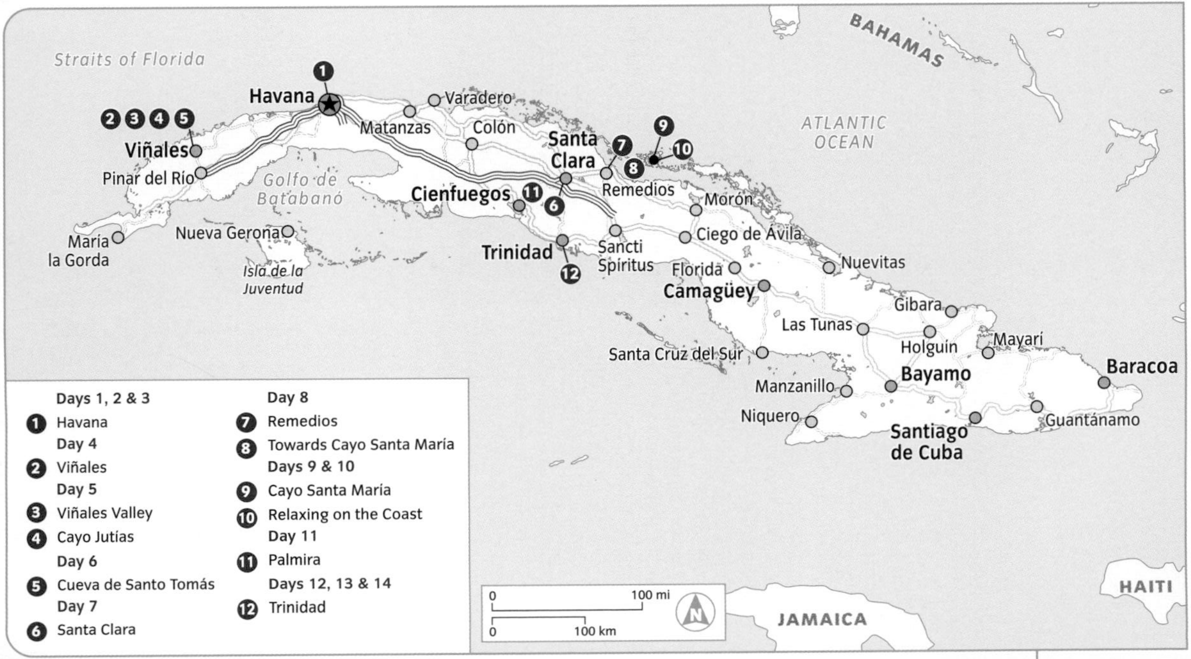

Flesh out the week tour of Cuba by spending longer in the island's cities and spreading out to discover a World Heritage site, more beaches, and another undeveloped Spanish colonial town. Make sure you squeeze in a snorkeling or walking trip around Viñales and fit in evenings in the music venues of Trinidad and Havana. This tour covers quite a lot of kilometers and you need to stay in accommodation in each of the towns. **START: Havana.**

Days One, Two, & Three

1 Havana. There are so many things to do and see in Havana, and street life to discover, that it's easy to fill three days in the city. *For a full tour of Havana, see p 88 in Chapter 6.*

Drive south out of Havana on Av. Independencia. At the spaghetti junction at Alturas de la Habana, turn right on Av. San Francisco (Calle 100). At a second spaghetti junction, turn west (left) onto the unsigned Autopista (A4) for Viñales. Just before Pinar del Rio, there's a sign marked Las Ovas to the (east/right). Take the western route, a winding cross-country shortcut to Viñales.

Day Four

2 Viñales. After checking into accommodation outside town or in a *casa particular* (private rooms for rent) in the town (p 109), visit the Centro de Visitantes (p 154) to plan

your excursions. Spend the rest of the afternoon wandering around the tranquil and pretty center before heading to the **Hotel Los Jazmines** (p 155) for a sunset drink overlooking the Viñales Valley. *See p 152.*

Day Five

3 Viñales Valley. Book an early morning walk through the Valley. Wander through paths amid the *mogotes* (limestone stacks covered in vegetation), watch oxen plough earth, and see and hear plenty of birds. If you visit during the tobacco season, the earth is carpeted in the verdant green of the tobacco plants. The valley floor is dotted with attractive *bohios* (farmers' huts) and *secadores* (drying houses for the tobacco leaf). These aren't so picturesque since the 2008 hurricanes ripped through the area tearing nearly all the *secadores* down; thatched roofs have been replaced by corrugated iron. *See also p 152.*

Viñales Valley.

Autopista Scam

Many visitors to Cuba hire a car in Havana and set off looking for the Autopista A1. Some spend three hours negotiating their way out of the city . . . others succumb to a scam. The Autopista isn't marked or easily identifiable because roads that most visitors would consider significant roads don't exist. Wily Cubans waiting for a lift (p 165) flag tourist cars down (identifiable by the T-branded red license plate) and offer to escort them to the correct turn off. One report Frommer's received suggested that the Cubans did escort the tourists to the right exit, but then demanded CUC$40 for their troubles. Another suggested that Cubans had returned them to the same (wrong) spot but still demanded CUC$20. To avoid the scam, drive down the road you believe is the Autopista and then ask somebody a couple of kilometers on. If you are on the wrong road, safe U-turns across the central reservation are made easy by the numerous breaks and very light traffic.

④ **Cayo Jutías.** Have lunch in town or set off for **Cayo Jutías,** a small key off the western coast, and dine at the beach restaurant there. Spend the afternoon sunbathing on the white sands or taking a small boat to visit **Starfish Beach** (p 52). *See p 51 and 68 for more on Cayo Levisa.*

Cueva de Santo Tomás.

Day Six
⑤ **Cueva de Santo Tomás.**
Get up early and, if you feel adventurous, take a horse ride through the valley, see the valley sights, or visit the **Cueva de Santo Tomás** (p 154). Those looking to kick-back amid the beautiful natural scenery should book into the **Rancho San Vicente hotel** for mud treatments or a dip in a thermal spring. Don't dally too long though, because you'll need to get to Santa Clara by nightfall. *See p 154.*

Drive back to Havana; at Alturas de La Habana there are traffic lights and the William Soler Hospital to orientate you on Calle 100. After the next spaghetti junction, take the left-hand road, the Primer Anillo de La Habana (first ring road). At the third spaghetti junction, turn east (right) for the Autopista Nacional (A1) to Santa Clara. The Primer Anillo de La Habana and the A1 aren't marked — buy a good road map, see p 105.

The historic town center, Remedios.

Day Seven
6 Santa Clara. Spend the day in Che Guevara's city. See **8** on p 18 and p 136.

Drive 49km (30 miles) north out of Santa Clara to Remedios. The correct (unsigned) turnoff from the Santa Clara ring-road is marked by a roundabout with flowering plants and a communist billboard at 2300, if you're traveling north. Take the left-hand turn here; the billboard should be passed on on your right.

Day Eight
7 Remedios. This is a quiet, well-preserved Spanish colonial town. Spend some time wandering around the small historic core before driving north to **Cayo Santa María.** *See also p 132.*

Exit at the north of town near the gas station and follow the road to Caibarién on the coast. Just outside Caibarién, a toll road (CUC$2 each way) leads you 50km (31 miles) along a causeway.

8 Towards Cayo Santa María.
It will take you some time to reach the cays, or rather collection of cays. Take time to admire the views from the causeway and look for water birds. Spend the afternoon getting acquainted with your resort (p 52) because the majority are quite large. If you aren't staying at **Villa Las Brujas,** you can stop for a drink at its bar overlooking the curved sweep of white sand.

Days Nine & Ten
9 Cayo Santa María. The cays here have some of the most brilliantly white sands in Cuba, and the waters are equally inviting. Spend the day sunbathing and drinking cocktails on the beach. Take a sunset catamaran ride with an open bar, music, and a lobster dinner.

10 Relaxing on the Coast.
Spend the morning at your hotel's spa before an afternoon on the water. Divers and fisherman can organize programs to suit their needs. Or, if you fancy a full day on the sea, opt for an organized seafari. In between drinking from the

Look out for water birds, such as herons at Cayo Santa Maria.

Autopista in the direction of Havana (that's west). Some 12km (7½ miles) west of Santa Clara take the signposted junction at Ranchuelo for the cross-country route south to **Cienfuegos** (p 124) via the pretty town of Palmira. The coastal road to Trinidad is signposted in town but there are several turnings required on the road to Trinidad that are unmarked. You will need to stop and ask.

open bar and listening to music, you can make snorkeling excursions off the boat to the barrier reef.

Day Eleven

⓫ Palmira. It will take you most of the day to drive south to Trinidad. Return to Santa Clara and negotiate your way (unsignposted) back to the

Days Twelve, Thirteen, & Fourteen

⓬ Trinidad. There's plenty to do in town, but if you have extra time or just fancy leaving the city, drive the 14km (8½ miles) south to **Playa Ancón** to relax on the white sands for the afternoon. Or, book a seafari on a boat at any of the hotels or tour agencies in town. If you're interested in the sugar drive, take the road 7km (4 miles) east to Sancti Spíritus and visit the fantastically green Valle de los Ingenios, a preserved sugar plantation with a slave-watching tower (p 149). *See p 146 for more on Trinidad, and* **⓫** *on p 55.* ●

Everyday Cuban Words & Phrases

Ahí Namá   There it is, that's it!

Bachata   Party, hanging out

Bárbaro   Great, fabulous

Chévere   Cool, excellent

Cirilo   Yes or yeah

Compañero/compañera   Literally, 'partner,' most common form of an address, as opposed to señor or señora, which are almost never used

Compay   Friend

Consumo   Price inclusive of food and drinks

Divisa   US dollar/Cuban Convertible Peso

Fanoso   Cheapskate

Fula   US dollar (slang)

Guajiro/Guajira   Peasant or farmer

Guarachar   To hang out or party

Por nada   You're welcome

Puro   Cuban cigar

¿Qué bolá?   'What's going on?' (slang)

Yuma   Street slang for the United States of America

3 The Best Special-Interest Tours

Spanish **Colonial Architecture**

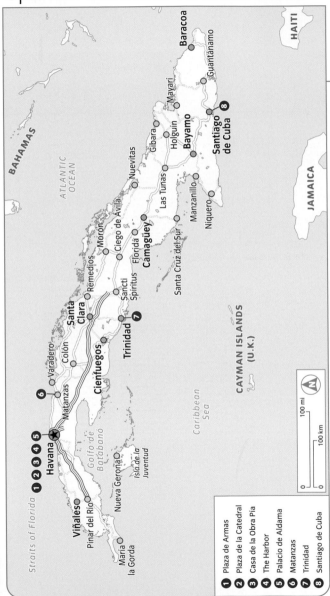

BAHAMAS

Straits of Florida

ATLANTIC OCEAN

HAITI

JAMAICA

Baracoa

Guantánamo

Mayarí

Gibara

Holguín

Bayamo

❽ Santiago de Cuba

Nuevitas

Las Tunas

Manzanillo

Níquero

Morón

Ciego de Ávila

Florida

Camagüey

Santa Cruz del Sur

Remedios

Santa Clara

Sancti Spíritus

Trinidad ❼

CAYMAN ISLANDS (U.K.)

Caribbean Sea

100 mi

100 km

Varadero

Colón

Cienfuegos

Matanzas ❻

Havana ❶❷❸❹❺

Golfo de Batabanó

Nueva Gerona

Isla de la Juventud

Viñales

Pinar del Río

María la Gorda

❶ Plaza de Armas
❷ Plaza de la Catedral
❸ Casa de la Obra Pía
❹ The Harbor
❺ Palacio de Aldama
❻ Matanzas
❼ Trinidad
❽ Santiago de Cuba

Cuba was conquered and settled by the Spaniards, who subsequently imported their architectural styles. From 1511, conquistador Diego Velázquez de Cuéllar founded the seven *villas* (towns) of Cuba. Fortresses, homes, and buildings centered around courtyards in the Mudéjar style and, in later years, baroque-influenced and neoclassical architecture, bloomed. Havana's Old City is the Spanish colonial prize and a UNESCO World Heritage Site. START: **Havana.**

❶ ★★★ **Plaza de Armas.** This is Havana's Spanish colonial core. At its eastern edge is the city's first fortress, the squat **Castillo de la Real Fuerza** dating from 1558–77 and built to protect the most important port in the New World (p 91). At the southern edge is the early neoclassical **El Templete** (built 1828) marking the founding of the city (p 91). Next to El Templete is the gloriously symmetrical **Casa del Conde de Santovenia** (now the Hotel Santa Isabel; p 100) with its creamy stone arches and *mediopunto* (stained-glass) windows. At the northern boundary is the **Palacio de los Capitanes Generales.** Built between 1776–91 (p 91), its ornamental flourishes embellish the facade; it's a fine example of baroque civic architecture. Almost as handsome is the neighboring **Palacio del Segundo Cabo** built at the same time. 🕐 *30 min to wander, 2 hrs at least for entry.*

❷ ★★★ **Plaza de la Catedral.** **The Catedral de San Cristóbal,** completed in 1777, displays an asymmetrical facade. Its undulating lines of baroque flourish dominate the pretty plaza. Opposite is the

Baroque facade of the Catedral, Havana.

plainer 18th-century **Casa del Conde Bayona** (now the Museo de Arte Colonial). The plaza is flanked by the exquisitely handsome **Palacio del Marqués de Aguas Claras** (now El Patio); the pretty **Palacio de Marqués de Arcos** that later became a post office; and the **Palacio del Conde Lombillo.** Most of these buildings were later adorned with covered arcades and/or extra

Mediapunto window, Matanzas.

Casa de la Obra Pía, Havana.

floors in accordance with the fashion. Just west of the square, the **Casa de la Condesa de la Reúnion** (now Fundación Alejo Carpentier) is another noted example of Cuban baroque. ⏱ *30 min to wander, 1 hr to include visit to the interior. Casa del Conde Bayona, C/ San Ignacio 61, Plaza de la Catedral; Palacio de Marqués de Arcos, Plaza de la Catedral, Palacio del Conde Lombillo, C/ Empedrado 151, Plaza de la Catedral; Fundación Alejo Carpentier, C/ Empedrado 215 e/ Cuba y San Ignacio).*

❸ **Casa de la Obra Pía.** One of the most noted examples of Cuban baroque architecture. It's adorned by a highly embellished facade imported from Spain in 1686. *Casa de la Obra Pía, C/ Obrapía 158 esq C/ Mercaderes.*

❹ **The Harbor.** Havana's defense became increasingly important and the small Castillo de la Real Fuerza (❶) was soon joined by the prominent **Castillo del Morro** (1589–1630). The city was designated the capital in 1607, and reinforcement soon came in the form of the long and dominant **La Fortaleza de San Carlos de la Cabaña** (1763–74). ⏱ *2–2½ hrs. See p 95 and 96.*

❺ ★★ **Palacio de Aldama.** Neoclassicism was developed in response to the elaborate decoration of the baroque style. Porticoes with columns, lintels, wrought iron decorative work, and functional items were embraced. The best example of

Spanish Decor

A wealth of architectural and decorative techniques adorn the interiors and exteriors of Cuba's buildings. *Mediapunto* are stained-glass windows positioned above wooden doors, introduced in the mid-18th century. Some of the best examples are found on the facade of the Casa del Conde de Bayona (see ❷ above) and the Hotel Santa Isabel (p 100). *Mamparas*, half door screens inlaid with plain or decorative glass, were installed in the houses of the rich. Wooden window grilles made of turned wood, known as *barrotes*, dating from the 18th century, were eventually replaced by plain or decorated wrought-iron grilles in the 19th century; grilles that divided neighbors' balconies called *guardevecinos* were installed. Dados made of decorative tiles paneled the lower walls; balconies were added to upper floors. Stone balustrades lining the roofs of mansions became common in the 19th century, and ornamental urns, such as those on the Palacio Junco in Matanzas, became a popular feature around the same time.

The Spanish Conquest

Diego Velázquez de Cuéllar set off to the West Indies with Cristóbal Colón on his second voyage in 1493–94. He helped conquer Cuba and became its governor in 1511. He founded Cuba's first seven *villas*. These were Nuestra Señora de la Asunción de Baracoa (1511); San Salvador de Bayamo (1513); la Santísima Trinidad (1514); Sancti Spíritus (1514); Santa María del Puerto Príncipe (now Camagüey) (1514); San Cristóbal de la Habana (1514); and Santiago de Cuba (1515).

neoclassicism in Havana is the Palacio de Aldama built for Don Domingo de Aldama in the 1840s and designed by Manuel José Carrera; it's fronted by a portal with Doric columns. *Av Simón Bolívar esq Amistad*.

6 ★ **Matanzas.** The **Teatro Sauto,** in the center of Matanzas, was designed by Italian architect Daniel Dall'Aglio. It's an excellent example of Cuban neoclassicism, built in 1863 for 300,000 pesos of gold (in today's value around US$600,000) and named after Ambrosio Sauto. Tradition says that Sauto cured the Queen of Spain, Isabella II, from genital herpes and thus became doctor to the Spanish court. He donated funds to build the theater. The marble decor comes from Carrara, Italy, the chairs from New York, and the lights from Paris. *See also p 129*.

7 ★★★ **Trinidad.** Trinidad is a treasure trove of preserved Spanish colonial architecture. Fine examples include the **Palacio de Justo Cantero** (now the history museum) dating from 1828–29 (p 148, **5**) and the beautifully proportioned 1812 **Palacio Brunet** (now the Romantic Museum; p 147, **2**). The pale yellow 1892 **Iglesia Parroquial** dominates the Plaza Mayor. (p 147, **1**). The sugar baron Sánchez Iznaga lived in the attractive blue house facing the

plaza (now the Museo de Arquitectura Colonial). *See p 147*, **3**.

8 ★★★ **Santiago de Cuba.** During the 17th and 18th centuries, the *Mudéjar* (Moorish influenced) style found in Spain was incorporated into Cuba's architecture. Carved and patterned ceilings, known as *alfarjes*, are good examples of the style. One of the best examples in the country can be found in the **Casa de Diego Velázquez (Museo de Ambiente Colonial Cubano).** Built between 1516 and 1530 it's an extraordinary example of the *Mudéjar* influence. Decorative window screens known as *celosias* cover the second floor. *See p 141*, **2**.

Windows of Casa de Diego Velázquez, Santiago.

Cuba's **1959** Revolution

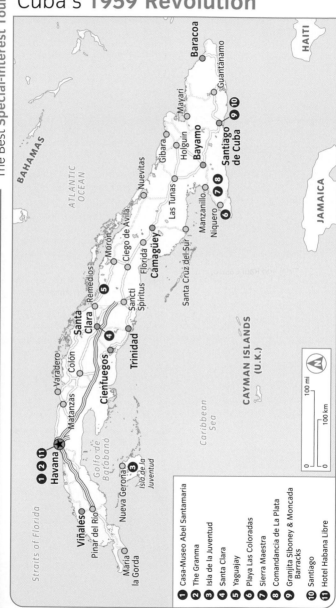

- BAHAMAS
- HAITI
- Baracoa
- Guantánamo
- Mayarí
- **❾ ❿**
- Gibara
- Holguín
- **Bayamo**
- **Santiago de Cuba**
- ATLANTIC OCEAN
- Nuevitas
- Las Tunas
- **❼ ❽**
- Manzanillo
- **❻**
- Niquero
- Ciego de Ávila
- Morón
- **❺** Remedios
- **Santa Clara**
- Sancti Spíritus
- Florida
- **Camagüey**
- Santa Cruz del Sur
- **❹**
- **Trinidad**
- **Cienfuegos**
- JAMAICA
- Colón
- Varadero
- Matanzas
- CAYMAN ISLANDS (U.K.)
- Caribbean Sea
- 100 mi
- 100 km
- Nueva Gerona
- **❸**
- Isla de la Juventud
- Golfo de Batabanó
- **❶ ❷ ⓫**
- **Havana**
- **Viñales**
- Pinar del Río
- María la Gorda
- Straits of Florida

1. Casa-Museo Abel Santamaria
2. The Granma
3. Isla de la Juventud
4. Santa Clara
5. Yaguajay
6. Playa Las Coloradas
7. Sierra Maestra
8. Comandancia de La Plata
9. Granjita Siboney & Moncada Barracks
10. Santiago
11. Hotel Habana Libre

For two years, a band of rebels waged war in the inaccessible terrain of the Sierra Maestra and eventually toppled the dictator Fulgencio Batista. The guerrillas were led by lawyer Fidel Castro, his brother Raúl, and Argentine doctor Ernesto (Che) Guevara. Their extraordinary story of determination and revolutionary ideals, aided by twists of fate and a growing network of poor rural farmers, led them to victory in January 1959. **START: Havana.**

❶ Casa-Museo Abel Santamaría. Inside this plain Vedado apartment in Havana, Fidel Castro and Abel Santamaria planned an assault on Santiago's military barracks in 1953. The apartment has been maintained as it was when used by Castro and is equipped with spartan furniture. ⏲ *15 min. C/ 25 164 e/ O y Infanta, Havana.* ☎ *7/835-0891. Free admission. Mon–Fri 10am–5pm, Sat 9am–1pm.*

❷ The Granma. In November 1956, Fidel and Raúl Castro, Ernesto (Che) Guevara, whom they had met in exile in Mexico, and a group of revolutionaries sailed to Cuba with weapons and an audacious plan: to overthrow, once and for all, the Batista government. They set sail from Mexico aboard the yacht *Granma*. The stealth journey was beset by all manner of hitches, including bad weather and scarce provisions. The *Granma* is now encased in glass at the **Museo de la Revolución** in Havana. The museum also details the history of the Revolution. *See p 94.*

❸ ★ Isla de la Juventud. Fidel Castro was imprisoned in the Presidio Modelo on the Isla de la Juventud following the 1953 assault on the Moncada Barracks (see **❾** below). He was sentenced to 15 years (brother Raúl was sentenced to 13 years). Castro wrote what was to become his 26th of July movement manifesto—*La Historia Me Absolverá* (*History will Absolve Me*). Under a Batista amnesty the Castro brothers were released in 1955 and went into exile in Mexico. Today, the prison is an eerie but fascinating museum. ⏲ *1 hr. 5km (3 miles) east of capital Nueva Gerona.* ☎ *46/32-5112. Admission CUC$2. Mon–Sat 8am–4pm, Sun 8am–noon.*

Military hardware marked by Fidel's guerrilla group name, exterior of Museo de la Revolución.

First peasant's home that Castro rebels came across, Playa Las Coloradas, Granma province.

4 Santa Clara. During the rebel campaign, Che Guevara's column had advanced west to Santa Clara. Guevara, along with Cienfuegos' troops, led the decisive battle that would take the town. His men derailed an armored train packed with Batista's troops, which can still be seen. Che Guevara is commemorated at his mausoleum in the city. *See p 138,* **6**.

5 Yaguajay. It was Commander Camilo Cienfuegos who led the column west to the Escambray mountains to take Santa Clara. In December 1958, to the north at Yaguajay, Cienfuegos succeeded in taking the garrison. A memorial and museum is dedicated to Cienfuegos. ⏱ *30 min. Museo Nacional Camilo Cienfuegos, Plaza de la Revolución Comandante Camilo Cienfuegos, Carretera a Vitoria.* ☎ *41/552689. Admission CUC$1. Mon–Sat 8am–4pm, Sun 9am–1pm.*

6 Playa Las Coloradas. Just 82 Castro rebels disembarked from the *Granma* close to Las Coloradas beach two days later than planned in December 1956, with few weapons and virtually no supplies. Batista forces had been tipped off to the

operation, and prompt aerial bombing killed about half the rebels; the others fled for the Sierra Maestra mountains in small groups. ⏱ *2–4 hrs. Parque Nacional Desembarco del Granma. Playa Las Coloradas, 13km (8 miles) south of Niquero. Admission CUC$5. Daily 7am–6pm.*

7 Sierra Maestra. After suffering an ambush, only 16 men remained, and when the survivors eventually met up at Cinco Palmas in the Sierra Maestra, only a dozen remained. They had eight rifles to their names. Against monumental odds, they nonetheless began to plan their offensive. Batista, no doubt convinced that the attempted sedition had been quashed, announced to the world that Fidel Castro and the other leaders had been killed and withdrew government forces from the area—a fatal mistake. Crafty Castro slowly but surely began to gain adherents and advance the cause of the 26th of July movement. A sign on the road from Niquero to Pilón marks the spot where Raúl Castro passed across a road in the Sierra Maestra.

8 ★★ Comandancia de La Plata. Fidel Castro and his band of rebels set up base in the Sierra Maestra. From here, Castro co-ordinated his rebel campaign, managing the four fronts he had established in the east of the country. ⏱ *3–4 hrs. Centro de Visitantes, Santo Domingo. 7.30–10am. Admission and guided hike CUC$12. See also p 63 and 96.*

9 ★★ Granjita Siboney & Moncada Barracks. On the night of 26th July 1953, 135 rebels made their way in vehicles from Granjita Siboney, a farmhouse just outside Santiago de Cuba, to the gates of the city's Moncada Barracks (p 142, **7**) in the city. Troops were shot at and more than 60 rebels were killed. Abel Santamaría was imprisoned

El Che

Che Guevara, born 14 June 1928, in Rosario, Argentina, to a middle-class family, set off on a motorcycle trip through the Americas in 1953, having just graduated in medicine. In 1954, he got caught in the crossfire of a CIA-supported overthrow of Guatemala's democratically-elected president Jacobo Arbénz. Exiled to Mexico after the coup, he met fellow exile Fidel Castro. The two hit it off, and soon Guevara was a principal figure in the Cuban revolutionary struggle. Despite chronic asthma and a weak constitution, Guevara was famous for his gritty work ethic and determination. He was later rewarded with high posts in the new government, including Minister of Industry and president of the National Bank.

Che soon tired of the politics and embarked on a crusade to spread the Revolution. In 1966 he went to Bolivia and began organizing a guerilla army. However, the United States military and CIA were already on his trail, and on 8th October, 1967, Guevara was caught by the Bolivian army, aided by US 'advisors.' Following consultations with Washington, he was executed.

and later killed. Fidel and Raúl escaped but were later captured and imprisoned on the Isla de la Juventud. The farmhouse contains furniture as well as bloodstained clothes and documents relating to the attack. ⏱ *15 min. Granjita Siboney, Carretera Siboney, Km 13.5. ☎ 22/39-9168. Admission CUC$1. Mon 9am–1pm, Tues–Sun 9.15am–4.45pm. See also p 142,* ❼.

❿ **Santiago.** Panicked by the news at Santa Clara, Batista fled the country on 1st January 1959. Fidel marched in to take Santiago de Cuba and gave a speech from the balcony of the town hall on **Parque Céspedes**. *See p 141.*

⓫ **Hotel Habana Libre.** On 8th January 1959 Fidel Castro marched into Havana. He installed his office in the Havana Hilton, renaming it the Habana Libre. In the foyer, there are photographs and exhibits relating to Revolution events. *See p 103.*

Granjita Siboney, Santiago de Cuba.

The Best Special-Interest Tours

Hemingway's **Cuba**

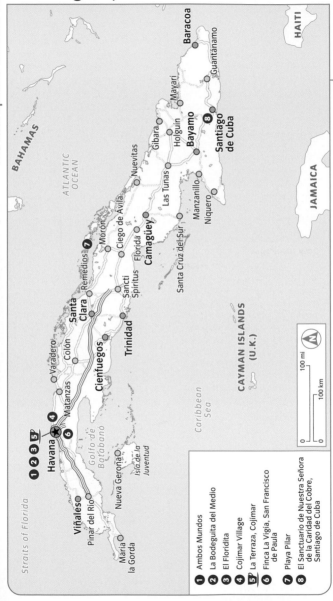

BAHAMAS

Straits of Florida

ATLANTIC OCEAN

María la Gorda

Pinar del Río

Viñales

Nueva Gerona

Isla de la Juventud

Golfo de Batabanó

Havana

Matanzas

Varadero

Colón

Cienfuegos

Trinidad

Santa Clara

Remedios

Sancti Spíritus

Morón

Ciego de Ávila

Florida

Camagüey

Santa Cruz del Sur

Las Tunas

Nuevitas

Manzanillo

Niquero

Gibara

Holguín

Mayarí

Bayamo

Santiago de Cuba

Guantánamo

Baracoa

HAITI

JAMAICA

Caribbean Sea

CAYMAN ISLANDS (U.K.)

100 mi

100 km

1. Ambos Mundos
2. La Bodeguita del Medio
3. El Floridita
4. Cojímar Village
5. La Terraza, Cojímar
6. Finca La Vigía, San Francisco de Paula
7. Playa Pilar
8. El Sanctuario de Nuestra Señora de la Caridad del Cobre, Santiago de Cuba

Ernest Hemingway (known as Papa) lived and worked at Finca La Vigía, south of Havana, from 1939 to 1960. He first stepped on Cuban soil in 1928 and, during subsequent visits, fell in love with Cuban culture; his passion for sailing and deep-sea fishing, a great source of his love affair with Cuba, is well documented. In July 1960 he left Cuba; he committed suicide in 1961 in the US.
START: **La Habana Vieja.**

① Ambos Mundos. Ernest Hemingway lived in a room at the Hotel Ambos Mundos in Old Havana between 1932 and 1939, during his many visits to Cuba. Hemingway claimed this was 'a good place to write,' and room no. 511 where he wrote parts of *For Whom the Bell Tolls* is a shrine to the late author. His bed, letters, and pictures are on display. ⏲ *20 min. C/ Obispo 153 esq C/ Mercaderes, La Habana Vieja.* ☎ *7/860-9530. Admission CUC$2. Daily 10am–5pm.*

② ★ La Bodeguita del Medio. The 'B del M,' as it's also known, oozes history and suffers from serious overcrowding in the tiny bar. Still, it's a must for any first-time trip to Havana because this is where Hemingway would stop while he lived at the Hotel Ambos Mundos. The collage of famous photos and signatures that crowd the walls here are legend. Tradition would have you start things off with a mojito, although they are notoriously weak here and unjustifiably expensive. Definitely order one with three- or five-year-old *añejo* rum if you plan on enjoying it. This place is crowded and rowdy, so don't come expecting anything less. There's live Cuban music in the squashed bar. *C/ Empedrado 207 e/ C/ San Ignacio and Cuba.* ☎ *7/867-1374.*

③ El Floridita. This is by far the classiest of the Hemingway hangouts in Havana, although it can get as crowded as La Bodeguita and is rowdier when there are tour groups

Hotel Ambos Mundos, Old Havana.

and live music. In fact, El Floridita is so upscale, I have a hard time imagining the rugged writer really enjoying this place. It costs you CUC$6 for a daiquiri in 'The Cradle of the Daiquiri'—be sure to get it shaken, not blended. The bartenders' deepred jackets blend perfectly with the plush decor. The long bar takes up a good portion of the front room, and there's quieter and more formal seating in the back. Most people, however, come here for the Hemingway association and to have their photograph taken next to the life-size bronze of the writer that props up the left-hand side of the

El Floridita, Havana.

bar. *C/ Obispo 557 esq C/ Monserrate.* ☎ *7/866-8856. www.floridita-cuba. com.*

4 Cojímar Village. Cojímar is an eastern suburb of Havana. Hemingway fished the sea off here with his boat the *Pilar* and its captain Gregorio Fuentes. Gregorio died in 2002 aged 104 but, until his death, he regaled tourists with his tales of Hemingway fishing expeditions. There's a bust of Hemingway overlooking the fort by the sea.

5 ★ La Terraza, Cojímar. The ghosts of Papa and his pal Gregorio are omnipresent here—just saunter through the swinging saloon-style doors and look around to admire the pictures. During high season, the small restaurant is somewhat unable to cope with its fame, but if you get here early or have a firm reservation, you don't have to wait to enjoy the well-prepared seafood, cool sea breezes, and a great view across the small plaza in Cojímar to the sea. The seafood paella is pretty good, and the lobster is usually fresh. *C/ 152 no. 161, Cojímar.* ☎ *7/ 766-5151. Mains CUC$6–25. MC, V. Daily lunch & dinner.*

6 ★ Finca La Vigía, San Francisco de Paula. Hemingway lived at Finca La Vigía between 1939 and 1960. His third wife, Martha Gellhorn, had found the property. You're not allowed into the home of the writer but can circle it and look at all the rooms through the windows. The house remains more or

La Terraza, Cojímar.

less as it was when Hemingway was living and writing here. There's a copious collection of books, paintings, and stuffed animal heads. In addition to an old typewriter, works of art by Picasso, Miró, and Klee are some of his more prized possessions. There's a small tower separate from the main house, which has some rooms with rudimentary exhibits, and you can even climb it for a better view all around. In the surrounding gardens, you can see Papa's pet cemetery and the author's dry-docked fishing boat, *Pilar*. ⏱ *1 hr. Carretera Central, Km 12.5. San Francisco de Paula.* ☎ *7/ 891-0809. Admission CUC$3. Camera CUC$5. Video CUC$50. Mon–Sat 10am–5pm, Sun 10am–1pm; closed when it's windy.*

Finca La Vigía, Ernest Hemingway's home.

➐ ★★★ Playa Pilar. The novelist was one of the first to explore Cayo Guillermo; in the 1930s and 1940s, Hemingway used to sail off the coasts of the northern cays in dogged pursuit of marlin and swordfish in the Atlantic. The celebrated beach on Cayo Guillermo, Playa Pilar, is even named for the author's beloved fishing boat, *Pilar*. In an episode befitting his macho, roguish character, Hemingway enlisted his crew and boat to hunt for Nazi submarines off Cuba's northern cays at the height of World War II (according to some, the island was awash with Nazi sympathizers and agents). Papa's companion was, as ever, Gregorio Fuentes, who some say was the model for the aged fisherman in *The Old Man and the Sea*, for which Hemingway won the 1953 Pulitzer Prize for Fiction. In Hemingway's novel *Islands in the Stream*, the main character looks longingly across the bay at Cayo Guillermo, asking rhetorically, 'See how green she is and full of promise?'. Evidently

the Cuban authorities, intent on developing the cays a half century after Hemingway first explored them, feel the same way. *See also p 74.*

➑ ★★ El Sanctuario de Nuestra Señora de la Caridad del Cobre, Santiago de Cuba. According to legend, the statue of Cuba's patron saint was discovered bobbing in the Bay of Nipe in 1611 by three young fishermen about to capsize in a storm. The Madonna wore a sign that read *yo soy la virgen de la caridad* (I am the Virgin of Charity). With the wooden statue in their grasp, the fishermen miraculously made it to shore. Hemingway—whose fisherman in *The Old Man and the Sea* made a promise to visit the shrine if he could only land his marlin—donated his Nobel Prize in Literature to the shrine, but it was stolen (and later recovered, but never again to be exhibited here). *Admission free. Daily 6am–6.30pm. See also p 143.*

Art Deco Architecture **in** Havana

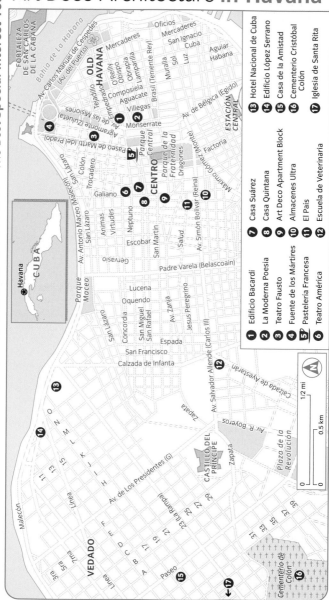

1 Edificio Bacardi
2 La Moderna Poesia
3 Teatro Fausto
4 Fuente de los Mártires
5 Pastelería Francesa
6 Teatro América
7 Casa Suárez
8 Casa Quintana
9 Art Deco Apartment Block
10 Almacenes Ultra
11 El País
12 Escuela de Veterinaria
13 Hotel Nacional de Cuba
14 Edificio López Serrano
15 Casa de la Amistad
16 Cementerio Cristóbal Colón
17 Iglesia de Santa Rita

Art Deco found its way to Havana in the late 1920s. A modern movement that stemmed from the Exposition Internationale des Arts Décoratifs et Industriales Modernes in Paris in 1925, it found expression in bricks and mortar between 1927 and the 1950s, in modified form. Decorative design such as geometric patterns and chevrons became *en vogue*. Throughout Havana, glorious examples can be found, in varying states of repair. START: La Habana Vieja.

1 ★★★ kids **Edificio Bacardí.** An outstanding example of Art Deco architecture, the rum empire's HQ stands on the edge of Old Havana. It was built in 1930 by Esteban Rodríguez Castells and **Rafael Fernández Ruenes.** Its ziggurat-style tower is crowned by the iconic Bacardí bat symbol and a 12-story facade is embellished by enameled terracotta. Note the bat symbol in the door panels and light shades in the café, the sun's rays adorning the elevator doors, and the letter B encased in wrought iron decoration. It's best photographed from the bar and sun terrace of the Hotel Plaza opposite. ⏱ *20 min. C/ Monserrate esq San Juan de Dios. See also Café Barrita, p 94.*

Edificio Bacardí exterior.

2 **La Moderna Poesia.** Walk two blocks south of **Edificio Bacardí.** The facade of the largest bookshop in Havana, **La Moderna Poesia,** is the Art Deco introduction to the top of Calle Obispo. It was designed by Ricardo Mira in 1941. *La Moderna Poesia, C/ Obispo esq Bernaza.*

3 **Teatro Fausto.** Cross Parque Central and walk down Prado. Just past the Moorish Hotel Sevilla is the imposing Teatro Fausto remodeled by Saturnino Parajón in 1938. It's a classic Art Deco design with a frieze of plant motifs branded across the upper structure and tile decoration in the foyer. More exciting, though, are the two Art Deco carved figures behind the theater on Calle Morro. *Teatro Fausto, Prado esq Colón.*

4 **Fuente de los Mártires.** Continue to the end of Prado. On the right, amid a small green park is a fountain. Cuba's most famous sculptor Rita Longa (1912–2000) designed the non-operational Fuente de los Mártires fountain (1941–47) that sits on the edge of Old Havana. *Fuente de los Mártires, Prado y Cárcel.*

5 **Pastelería Francesa.** This French-style patisserie, with seats outside facing the Parque Central or inside amid the pastel pink décor, serves a good range of croissants, pain au chocolat, and pain au raisin with a small selection of savory items. *Prado 410 e/ Neptuno y San Rafael.* ☎ *7/862-0739. $.*

The colorful Casa Quintana.

6 ★★★ Teatro América. The Teatro América dates from 1941. It sits beneath a large block of apartments known as the Rodríguez Vázquez building, designed by Fernando Martínez Campos and Pascual de Rojas on the principal north-south road in Centro. The Art Deco theater sign on the exterior is just the beginning; this is an architectural gem. The foyer floor is designed in a circle of zodiac symbols and the exquisite highlight is the preserved ladies' cloakroom area. It's theatrical and stylized, with blue furniture, green wall panels, and lamps. ⏱ *20 min. C/ Galiano 253 y Concordia.*

7 Casa Suárez. An outstanding example of Art Deco, built in 1934. Note the enormous stylized lamps flanking the main doorway. *C/ Aguila esq San Miguel.*

8 ★ Casa Quintana. On Calle Galiano stands the colorful 1937 facade of Casa Quintana by Alejandro Capó Boada. *Casa Quintana, Galiano e/ San Rafael y San Miguel.*

9 Art Deco Apartment Block. Further along on a prominent corner is a beige block of apartments with striking balconies. *Galiano esq Zanja.*

10 Almacenes Ultra. On Calzada de la Reina, this run-down former shop sports characteristic typography and flower motifs. *Almacenes Ultra, Calzada de la Reina 109 e/ Rayo y Angeles.*

11 El País. Close by is the glass-fronted former El País newspaper building, by Cristóbal Díaz and Rafael de Cárdenas. The frieze work is by Cándido Alvarez. *El País building, C de la Reina 158 e/ Rayo y San Nicolás.*

12 Escuela de Veterinaria. The front doors of the University of

Striking balconies on an apartment building, corner of Galiano esq Zanja, Centro.

Havana's Veterinary School in Vedado are locked, but this just gives you a chance to admire the carved bronze animals embedded in its large doors. On top of the structure are the small Art Deco heads of carved horses, by Manuel Tapial Ruano dated 1943. *Av Ayestarán and Carlos III.*

⓭ ★ Hotel Nacional de Cuba.
The 12-storey Hotel Nacional was designed by McKim, Mead & White from New York, and completed in 1930. It has become one of the iconic symbols of Havana. Its exterior is decorated with bands of Art Deco nature motifs.

Opposite is an apartment building on Calle O y 21 exhibiting Art Deco typography and nature motifs. *C/O e/ 21 y 23.*

⓮ ★ Edificio López Serrano.
Designed by Ricardo Mira and Miguel Rosich in 1932, this gray, 12-story imposing block of apartments is topped by four storeys in ziggurat style. Its facade has been decorated with plant motifs and there are large stylized plant pots lining open areas. Inside is a decorative nickel silver art deco panel, *El Tiempo*, by Enrique García Cabrera. *C13 esq L.*

⓯ ★★★ Casa de la Amistad.
This was once the residence of beauty queen and socialite Catalina Lasa and landowner Juan Pedro Baró. The exterior is mock-Italian Renaissance but some of the unusual and attractive interiors are Art Deco. Off the main hall are the Art Deco dining room, and the masonry work in what is now the café is a wonder. The curving staircase is a visual delight. *Casa de la Amistad, Paseo 406 e/ 17 y 19. Daily 8am–5pm.*

⓰ ★★★ Cementerio Cristóbal Colón. Inside the cemetery are

Catalina Lasa-Juan Pedro Baró mausoleum.

some Art Deco tomb highlights. The **Catalina Lasa-Juan Pedro Baró mausoleum** dating from 1936 looks like a space-age tomb. The doors of this enormous mausoleum were exquisitely designed by René Lalique and feature two angels, enormous wings outstretched, kneeling in prayer opposite each other. Famous Cuban sculptor Rita Longa designed the Art Deco melancholy marble *piedad* (pietà) that adorns the Aguilera family tomb.

Note also the pantheon of sugar baron Andrés Gomez Mena at the entrance to the cemetery and the ethereal angel on the frieze band. ⏱ *1–2 hrs. C/ Zapata and 12.* ☎ *7/832-1050. Admission CUC$1. Daily 8am–5pm.*

⓱ Iglesia de Santa Rita. This modern church designed by Victor Morales contains the 1943 Art Deco plaster statue Saint Rita de Cascia by Cuba's famous sculptor, Rita Longa. *Av 5 esq C/ 26.*

A **Musical Tour of Cuba**

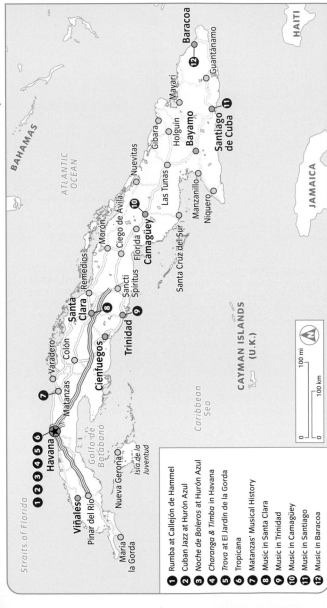

1. Rumba at Callejón de Hammel
2. Cuban Jazz at Hurón Azul
3. *Noche de Boleros* at Hurón Azul
4. *Charanga & Timba* in Havana
5. *Trova* at El Jardin de la Gorda
6. Tropicana
7. Matanzas' Musical History
8. Music in Santa Clara
9. Music in Trinidad
10. Music in Camagüey
11. Music in Santiago
12. Music in Baracoa

The seductive sounds of richly percussive Cuban music are, in many people's minds, the country's greatest export. Within Cuba, music seeps out of cafés and Casas de la Trova in the mid-afternoon and thunders out of dance halls at night. The musical diet is a dizzying menu of styles with uncommon appeal, so emphatically tropical that you can almost hear the humidity in the vocals, chords, and percussion. This mix of salsa, rumba, mambo, *son, danzón* (a dance-hall style), and *cha-cha-chá* stems from the rich blend of African, Spanish, French, and Haitian cultures. The roots of contemporary Cuban popular music lie in the 19th century's combination of African drums and rhythms along with Spanish guitar and melody. Most forms of Cuban music feature Latin stringed instruments, African bongos, congas, and claves (wooden percussion sticks), and auxiliary instruments such as maracas and *guiros*.

❶ ★★★ Rumba at Callejón de Hammel. Rumba is the most intensely African music of Cuba, an outgrowth of Afro-Cuban religion and slave music. Based on percussion and voice, it features call-and-response in both African languages and Cuban Spanish. There are three primary variations: *yambú*, which is the slowest; *guaguancó*, with a relaxed mid-tempo feel; and *Columbia*, which is the most frenetic. This outdoor venue is the best place in Havana to see and feel the energy.

Elsewhere in Havana, the unmissable **Sábado de la Rumba,** a mesmerizing Afro-Cuban show, takes place at **El Gran Palenque.** *Callejón de Hammel, e/ C/ Espada y Aramburu. Sun at noon. Free admission. El Gran Palenque. C/ 4 e/ Calzada and Av 5, Vedado. Admission CUC$5. Sat at 3pm.*

❷ ★★ Cuban Jazz at Hurón Azul. Cuban jazz, incorporating sophisticated Afro-Cuban elements, is highly rated in international jazz circles. Two of the genre's big names are the pianists Chucho Valdés and Gonzalo Rubalcaba. Jazz can be heard here.

Rumba at Callejón de Hammel, Centro, Havana.

Sounds of *Son*

The perennial form of Cuban traditional music is *son* (literally, 'sound' and pronounced sohn), a style of popular dance music that originated in El Oriente in the early 1900s. Though it was born of miscegenation, *son's* development in the 20th century encountered very little of the cross-fertilization of genres that normally takes place. *Son* thus remains a traditional and pure indigenous style of music. African rhythm instruments (most notably the bongos and maracas) combine with the Cuban tres, a small, high-pitched guitar featuring three sets of double strings. Giants of *son* include Trio Matamoros, Ignacio Pineiro, and Sexteto Habanero, and the individuals who formed the Buena Vista Social Club. The percussive swing of *son* can be heard in many newer types of Cuban music and it forms one of the lynchpins of modern salsa.

There's also an international jazz festival organized by Chucho Valdés (p 159). *Hurón Azul, C/ 17 esq H, Vedado.* ☎ *7/832-4551. Admission CUC$1. Second Thursday of the month at 5pm.*

❸ ★★ *Noche de Boleros* at **Hurón Azul.** Boleros are slow-paced romantic ballads popular in Havana, and in other music venues across the island (see p 145). They can also be heard at the **Festival Internacional Boleros de Oro** in June. *Hurón Azul, C/ 17 esq H, Vedado.* ☎ *7/832-4551. Admission CUC$1.Sat 10pm. See also p 43.*

❹ ★★★ *Charanga & Timba* in **Havana.** The style of *songo* was created by members of Los Van Van, one of the most popular Cuban bands since the 1970s. The rhythm was largely the brainchild of drummer 'Changuito' (José Luis Quintana) and bassist Juan Carlos Formell, who fused the funky grooves of Motown's James Jamerson with a traditional style known as *charanga*. The innovations of Los Van Van led directly to *timba*, the rowdiest style to date. This heavily amplified dance music displays a mature knowledge

of jazz, hip hop, and funk, and folkloric Afro-Cuban styles. Leading groups include NG La Banda, Bamboleo, Charanga Habanera, and Klimax.

Most of these groups play at Egrem-run (state-run recording company) venues in Havana on a regular basis. See http://promociones. egrem.co.cu/ for the weekly line up. Also check the *cartelera* (weekly line-up) in front of the **Salon Rojo, Vedado,** a fashionable music venue.

❺ ★★ *Trova* at **El Jardín de la Gorda.** *Trovas* are ballads that have been performed since colonial days. The *nueva trova* is a style of acoustic, politically motivated music that arose after the 1959 Revolution, coincident with *nueva canción* (new song) throughout Latin America. The biggest stars of *nueva trova*, still hugely popular throughout the Spanish-speaking world, are Silvio Rodríguez and Pablo Milanés. Newer proponents to look for include Santiago Feliú, Amaury Pérez, Sara González, and Carlos Varela. *Centro Iberoamericano de la Décima, C/ A e/ 25 y 27, Vedado.*

Tropicana, Havana.

☎ *7/837-5383. Free admission. Third Sun of the month. 5pm.*

6 ★★★ **Tropicana.** It's all that you could ever hope to imagine. In a swirl of high heels, feathered head-dresses, and outrageous colorful costumes, the dancing and choreographic extravaganza begins. It's a fantastic spectacle, hugely enjoyable, and very flamboyant. *See also p 110. C/ 72 e/ C/41 and 45, Mariano.* ☎ *7/267-0110. www.cabaret-tropicana.com.*

7 **Matanzas' Musical History.** *Danzón*, a dance and musical form that evolved from the contradanza performed by Haitian and French immigrants in the late 19th century, is a lyrical European dancehall style played by *orquestas*. The first *danzón* was originally composed and played in Matanzas in 1879 by Miguel Faílde. Unfortunately the location of his creation, the **Sala de Conciertos José White** (the White Center) on Calle 79 e/ 288 y 290, is now closed for repairs, and no date has been set for reopening. Matanzas was also the birthplace of rumba; perhaps the best-known rumba group in Cuba, now in its

Buena Vista Social Club

In the late 1990s, a series of records and a documentary film brought a group of aging Cuban musicians to the world's attention. The unexpected popularity abroad of the Buena Vista Social Club and its individual artists—Ibrahim Ferrer, Compay Segundo, Rubén González, Eliades Ochoa, and Omara Portuondo—made traditional Cuban sounds very much in demand throughout Cuba and internationally. Buena Vista and company, though, is only the latest round of Cuban music to circle the globe, echoing the earlier mambo and *cha-cha-chá* crazes that took the United States and Europe by storm in the 1950s. Omara Portuondo can often be heard singing in Havana. She normally performs at the Salon 1930 hall in the Hotel Nacional de Cuba, and has also sung at Teatro América.

Orchestral Maneuvers

Cuba's musical heritage centers around a number of instruments. Generally known outside of Cuba as congas, *tumbadoras* are tall, conical drums typically played by seated musicians. Three similar-looking *tumbadoras* are employed in rumba music. In a contemporary mambo or salsa group, two or three *tumbadoras* are simultaneously played by a single musician. By varying the shape and position of their hands, *congueros* (conga players) are able to elicit an impressive variety of sounds from each drum. *Timbales* are two metal drums, about the size of snare drums and are mounted on a single stand. They are known as *macho* (smaller and higher in pitch) and *hembra* (larger and lower in pitch). This instrument evolved from classical music's tympani, and was first used in *danzón*. Bongos consist of two wooden drums—also known as *macho* and *hembra*—that are joined in the center of each shell. Typically made of rawhide cylinders filled with seeds or beads, *maracas* are usually played by background singers. The *guiro* is a handheld instrument that is simply a hollowed-out gourd. A thin stick is dragged along grooves that have been carved into the side, yielding a distinctive tone. The *chekeré* is a large, circular gourd surrounded by beads fixed onto net-like strings.

third generation, is the legendary Muñequitos de Matanzas. The Columbia rumba style (see ❶) was developed by railway workers on this line between Havana and Matanzas.

Catch the Orquestra Sinfónica de Matanzas at Teatro Sauto.

Music and dance, including performances of the Orquesta Sinfónica de Matanzas, can be seen at the **Teatro Sauto** (p 129) as it waits for its return to the White Center.

❽ **Music in Santa Clara.** The musical scene in Santa Clara is low key. There's an eclectic line up at the town's most popular spot, **Club Mejunje,** that's a must for gay visitors. **Bar La Marquesina,** just off the main square, hosts good *son* bands nightly. *See p 138.*

❾ ★★ **Music in Trinidad.** Trinidad boasts a variety of music venues all within a stone's throw of each other. On the steps next to the church, **La Escalinata,** live bands play nightly. The action later moves to the top of the steps and converts to a disco in the back building (the Casa de la Música). The real highlight though is the energetic dance

Palenque de los Congos Reales, Trinidad.

❿ Music in Camagüey. The Casa de la Trova facing Parque Agramonte is one of the most attractive *trova* venues in the country, with a long courtyard and covered terracing in a Spanish colonial home. Its line-up features a mix of styles but *son* groups feature consistently. *C/ Salvador Cisneros 171.* ☎ *32/29-1357. Admission CUC\$3 Tues–Thurs noon–6pm, 9pm–midnight, Fri, Sat noon–6pm, 9pm–1am, Sun 11am–4pm, 9pm–1am.*

⓫ ★★★ Music in Santiago. Rumba is prominently featured in carnival celebrations in Santiago de Cuba. *Son* and *trova* can be heard at the city's three main venues (p 141). Look out for groups such as Septeto Santiaguero and Sones de Oriente.

The highly talented **Ballet Folklórico Cutumba** (see p 145) remains one of Cuba's outstanding music and dance groups. Music and dance can also be seen during the city's annual popular Carnival del Caribe also known as Fiesta del Fuego. *Santiago's Carnival is one week pivoting around 26 July. See also p 145. Fiesta del Fuego is held*

extravaganzas by Afro-Cuban *grupo folklóricos* (folkloric groups) at the open-air patio of **Palenque de los Congos Reales.** *Casa de la Música, C/ Fco Javier Zerguera s/n.* ☎ *41/99-3414. egremtdad@enet.cu Admission free. Daily 10am–2.30am. Palenque de los Congos Reales, C Fernando H. Echerri. Admission CUC\$2. Sun–Fri 1.30pm–midnight, Sat 1.30pm–1am.*

Nengón and Kiribá, Baracoa.

Claves

The heartbeat of Cuban music is the clave, which refers to a distinctive rhythm and the instrument. The instrument is comprised of two thick cylinders of wood, usually about 17½ cm (7 inches) long. Although the actual instrument isn't necessarily played in every song, all Cuban rhythms are built up from the concept of the *clave*. There's a sophisticated theory surrounding this five-note beat—a repetitive, two-bar pattern with two slight variations: the *son clave*, the basis of folkloric and popular styles such as *son*, *son montuno*, and mambo; and the *rumba clave*, the basis of folkloric and religious styles with a more distinctly syncopated and African flavor, especially the percussion-and-vocal music known as rumba. More than an instrument, *la clave* is in a sense the paradigm behind all Afro-Cuban music. The particular variation (*rumba clave* or *son clave*) and the 'direction' of the *clave* (meaning which bar of the two-bar pattern is played first) determine what the other instruments can and cannot do; it even determines what the more attuned dancers do.

across seven days between the first and second week of July. www.casa delcaribe.cult.cu/.

⓬ ★★★ Music in Baracoa. Both *Nengón* and *Kiribá* are early Cuban musical genres that predate *son*. Both incorporate simple rhythms that emerged from the Baracoa and Guantánamo areas. The only place you can hear this music and see

accompanying dancing is by organizing a fiesta. It's a festive occasion where local food, one of the best spreads in Cuba, is served.

In addition, Baracoa's cosy **Casa de la Trova** is one of the best on the island. *Grupo Kiribá y Nengón (Teresa Roché. ☎ 21/64-3447). Cost: by donation. Three days' notice is required. Casa de la Trova, see* *p 145.* ●

4 The Great **Outdoors**

Best **Beaches**

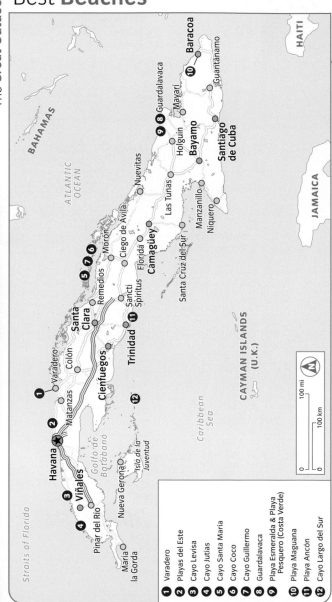

1 Varadero
2 Playas del Este
3 Cayo Levisa
4 Cayo Jutías
5 Cayo Santa María
6 Cayo Coco
7 Cayo Guillermo
8 Guardalavaca
9 Playa Esmeralda & Playa Pesquero (Costa Verde)
10 Playa Maguana
11 Playa Ancón
12 Cayo Largo del Sur

Cuba has always attracted sun-hunting visitors to its white-sand, palm-tree studded beaches. Those along the north coast slope gently into sparkling turquoise Caribbean waters. The only beaches that don't match the image of the tropical idyll are a couple of fine-black volcanic sand on the southeastern coast.

① ★ **kids** **Varadero.** Cuba's premier and most popular beach destination, Varadero is the common name for the entire length of the **Hicacos Peninsula.** The peninsula, which takes its name from a local spiny cactus, is 23km (14 miles) long, with a nearly continuous medium band of fine white sand. Backed by mangroves and the calm waters of Cárdenas Bay, the peninsula is less than a mile across at its widest point.

Home to indigenous populations and a base camp for itinerant Taíno and Carib fishermen, Varadero was largely ignored throughout the Spanish colonial period. Although it was first developed in 1887 as a summer retreat by 10 families from Cárdenas, its real potential as a tourist destination was realized relatively late. The first hotel was built here in 1910, and US industrial magnate Irénée Dupont built his **Mansión Xanadú** here in 1928 (p 18). A small cadre of celebrities and gangsters followed, including Al Capone. Still, at the time of the Revolution, there were only three hotels in Varadero. Today, there are more than 55, with large resorts occupying a large share of the peninsula. See also Chapter 5, p 75.

Varadero beach.

② **Playas del Este.** Slightly less polished than Varadero are these small, white-sand beaches with a handful of watersports facilities just 15–20 minutes from downtown Havana. There's a clutch of hotels and *casas particulares* (private rooms for rent) in the small towns of Santa María del Mar and Guanabo.

③ ★ **Cayo Levisa.** The small tropical island of Cayo Levisa is fronted by a bright-white curve of fine sand; charming hotel cabins dot its beach. It's a rare find in terms of peace and low-impact accommodation. Diving, watersports and bird-watching are

Travel Tip

Cuba's beaches don't come with any public restroom facilities. As most beaches are backed by resorts, you will need to ask inside the hotels if you're not staying nearby.

Cayo Levisa.

excellent. The island is part of the Archipiélago de los Colorados, which includes **Cayo Paraíso**, an even smaller island reputed to have been a favorite fishing haunt of Ernest Hemingway.

④ Cayo Jutías. Connected to the mainland by a causeway, this small beach is made up of pristine white sands and crystal-clear aquamarine waters. If you're feeling adventurous, walk south to **Playa Las Estrellas** (Star Fish beach) passing wild and isolated sands and

Cayo Jutías.

driftwood formed into weird and creative sculptures. A new nautical center offers boat excursions to Starfish Beach, nearby Isla Mégano, and diving. *See also p 68.*

⑤ ★★★ Cayo Santa María. Also known as la Cayería del Norte, this small string of tiny islands, mangrove swamps, and coral reefs has some of the most attractive beaches in Cuba (although a huge hotel megacity at its northernmost point may not keep it so beautiful for long).

The beaches on both **Cayo Las Brujas** and **Cayo Santa María** are spectacular, but the premier sites are **Playa Ensenachos** and **Playa Mégano** on Cayo Ensenachos. The protected waters here are crystal clear, and you can usually wade out a couple hundred meters without the water getting much above your waist. However, these once public beaches are now the exclusive domain of guests at the Royal Hideaway Ensenachos. If you make it up here without staying in one of the six hotels, public beaches include La Salina, Punta Madrugilla, which is good for snorkeling, and Perlas Blancas.

⑥ ★★★ kids Cayo Coco. The cays are part of the **Archipiélago**

Beach Politics

Until February 2008, Cubans were not permitted to stay in the all-inclusive resort areas of Cuba. Although, in theory, they now can, most don't have the money for such luxuries. In toll-gated areas, Cubans have to buy a pre-arranged CUC$10 lunch voucher in order to spend the day on the beach. With salaries running at CUC$10–20 a month, this kind of excursion is prohibitive. Cuba's beach resort areas are stunningly beautiful in the main, but they are also devoid of genuine Cuban culture. The majority of the resorts haven't evolved from pre-existing towns, and so have no real local residents. Cuban workers and Cuban culture (in a debased form) are brought in on a daily basis. However, thousands of Cubans working in these resorts rely on tourists' tips to augment meager salaries.

de Sabana-Camagüey, which extends 300km (186 miles) along the north coast and consists of around 400 large islands and small cays. Cayos Coco and Guillermo (**7**), the most developed of the entire stretch, are populated by just a handful of resort hotels—although more are planned on Cayo Coco. Both islands are reached by a 27km (17 miles) *pedraplén* (a human-built causeway) from the mainland.

The unspoiled beaches have spectacular white, powdery sand and the waters are a classic Caribbean-style crystalline turquoise. Cayo Coco is the better known of the two cays, probably due to its earlier development. The best-known Cayo Coco beaches are **Playa Larga** and **Playa Colorada**—gentle strips of perfect white sand lapped by brilliant greeny-blue; **Playa Los Flamencos,** a few kilometers west, is a slightly more isolated (but not for much longer) and a quieter beach, and beyond this is **Playa Prohibida.** Together, they're among the stellar beaches of Cuba.

7 ★★★ **kids** Cayo Guillermo. The cay's beaches—**Playa El Paso, Playa del Medio,** and **Playa**

Larga—are every bit as spectacular as those on Cayo Coco; in fact, at low tide, the waters are so shallow that you can wade out several hundred meters, making them preferable to the beaches on Cayo Coco for youngsters. The landscape is similar to Cayo Coco, but Guillermo boasts the most spectacular beach of either cay, and perhaps the entire northern coastline: **Playa Pilar,** long ago explored by Ernest Hemingway (p 37). It's pure and unadulterated white sand, azure seas, and the odd scudding white cloud.

A third cay—east of Cayo Coco—**Cayo Romano,** and the beaches out on **Cayo Paredón Grande** (tiny despite its name), are undeveloped.

Travel Tip

Most of Cuba's beach hotels have their own catamarans, sailboards, and other facilities for watersports. Kite surfing and paragliding are also sometimes possible.

8 ★★ **kids** Guardalavaca. The finest, and really the only, resort

Playa Guardalavaca.

area on the eastern half of the island remains charmingly low-key. Its rural and somnolent past is reflected in the resort's poetic name, which literally means 'watch the cow.' Today that moniker evokes a pastoral setting that hardly seems consistent with the coterie of full-fledged, all-inclusive resort hotels that gaze out over some of the finest beaches in Cuba.

❾ ★★ Playa Esmeralda & Playa Pesquero (Costa Verde). These are the two newest and most exclusive beaches on the island. The backdrop is a bucolic region thick with sugar-cane fields, grazing cattle, and luxuriant, rolling hills sprinkled with royal palms. *See p 86.*

Birds of Paradise

The cayos' natural gifts are some of the best in Cuba: nearly 400km (250 miles) of coral reefs, plus an ecotourist's bundle of lagoons, marshes, and one of Cuba's most abundant populations of birds, with more than 150 species. The latter include the Americas' largest native colony of pink flamingos, estimated at upwards of 10,000 birds, which often appear as a gauzy pink haze shimmering on the horizon (except in May, when they venture close to the causeway), as well as herons, pelicans, black and white egrets, white ibis, and other tropical species. The waters off the cays are flush with grouper, snapper, and mackerel, while deeper off the coast, fishermen catch marlin and swordfish.

Paradise Found

Christopher Columbus first sailed around the coast at Guardalavaca, landing just to the west at the Bay of Bariay in late 1492. He declared it 'the most beautiful land that human eyes have ever seen.' Columbus may have been given to hyperbole, repeatedly touting the unrivaled virtues of the places where he dropped anchor, but his assessment of Guardalavaca remains accurate. The area was originally home to several indigenous groups, and today it's recognized as Cuba's archaeological capital, primarily for the discovery of the 15th-century Taíno Indian village and burial site near Guardalavaca, one of the most important pre-Columbian sites in the Caribbean. The *bohíos* (thatched roof huts) that dot the thickly wooded hills still evoke that Caribbean discovery 500 years later.

⓾ ★ Playa Maguana. About 22km (14 miles) from Baracoa on the very bad road to Moa, this quiet beach is popular with day-trippers and locals. The sea can slope quite steeply and the greenish waters are flecked with midnight blue. There's also a small hotel with a private cove. *See p 115.*

⓫ ★ Playa Ancón. Though it can't quite compare with Cuba's prettiest and most prestigious beaches, Playa Ancón is still a beautiful beach with one distinct advantage over those other, isolated stretches of sand: proximity to Trinidad. Just 13km (8 miles) from town, Ancón, a 3-km (2-mile) strip at the end of a peninsula, is a quick and easy ride to and from Trinidad, so beach lovers can stay here and visit the colonial wonder of Trinidad at their will.

Both the Brisas del Mar Trinidad and Playa Ancón hotels, as well as the major travel agencies in town, offer diving and snorkeling excursions as well as watersports. Local operators also offer seafari expeditions to **Cayo Blanco,** with boat trips to the island, lunch, and snorkeling. Trips depart from the Marina Naútica Marlin. Tour operator Cubanacán runs trips. *C/ José Martí e/ C/ Francisco Javier Zerquera y C/ Colón,* ☎ 41/99-6142.

⓬ ★★★ kids Cayo Largo del Sur. Cayo Largo del Sur—or more simply, Cayo Largo—is the second-largest island in the Archipiélago de los Canarreos, and the only other island in the chain to support any population or tourism activity. The island's primary attraction is its uninterrupted kilometers of pristine white-sand beach, considered the best in Cuba. The island also provides fabulous scuba-diving and snorkeling opportunities, excellent wildlife viewing, and great bonefish, tarpon, and deep-sea fishing.

Cayo Largo has a long and rich history as a stomping and fishing ground for nomadic Caribe and Siboney indigenous populations. It was also visited by Christopher Columbus on his second voyage in 1494, and used as a base and stop-over point by pirates and corsairs, including Sir Francis Drake, Henry Morgan, and Jean Lafitte.

Best **Diving**

Straits of Florida

BAHAMAS

Havana
Viñales

Santa Clara

ATLANTIC OCEAN

Cienfuegos ⑥

① ② ③

Trinidad

Camagüey

④

Baracoa

Bayamo

⑦

Santiago de Cuba

Caribbean Sea

CAYMAN ISLANDS (U.K.)

⑤

❶	María La Gorda
❷	Isla de la Juventud
❸	Cayo Largo
❹	Jardines de la Reina
❺	Cayo Coco y Guillermo
❻	Bay of Pigs
❼	Santiago de Cuba Province

```
0        100 mi
0      100 km
```

Cuba has prime diving sites scattered around its entire coastline. Despite the fact that access to all the destinations is easier now than in previous years, Cuba's standards may still not be up to your own: serious divers may wish to bring their own equipment.

❶ ★★★ **María La Gorda.** More than 50 dive sites are within a 1-hour boat ride of this resort. Visibility is excellent and the waters of the bay here stay calm year-round, making entry and exit a breeze. Expect to see fabulous coral and sponge formations, colorful tropical fish, turtles, eels, barracuda, and rays on your dive. *Villa María La Gorda,* ☎ *48/77-8077. www.gaviota-grupo.com. See also p 68.*

❷ ★★★ **Isla de la Juventud.** The diving here is simply wonderful. The waters are crystal clear, and

there are walls, corals, caves, and even a few wrecks. Most trips head to **Punta Francés,** a national maritime park. *Centro Internacional de Buceo Colony,* ☎ *46/39-8181.*

❸ ★★★ **Cayo Largo.** With rich coral reefs, steep walls, and numerous wrecks, Cayo Largo has excellent scuba diving. Whale sharks can be seen around October and November and at a new dive site, **Cayo Blanco,** it's now possible to dive with dolphins. *International Dive Center,* ☎ *45/24-8214. buceo.marina@repgc.cls.tur.cu. Avalon*

(Italian-owned dive and fishing operator), ☎ 5/86-1818. www.divingin cuba.com. *With accommodation, Villa Marinera.*

❹ ★★ Jardines de la Reina.

Under the hundreds of uninhabited virgin cays lie 80 dive sites that offer the possibility of seeing whale sharks, hammerhead sharks, bull sharks, and hawksbill turtles, among others. Whale shark high season runs August through January, with the peak months being October–December. *Avalon (www.divingin cuba.com) runs seven-day diving packages on three live-aboard boats or a floating hotel, La Tortuga.*

❺ Cayo Coco y Guillermo.

There are a couple of dozen dive sites, including five superior sites, easily accessible from the cays. They range in depth from 5 to 40m (16–130 feet). Corals, rays, and turtles can be seen. *Blue Diving* ☎ *33/30-8180 at Meliá Cayo Coco. Marlin Marina at Cayo Guillermo,* ☎ *33/30-1737.*

❻ ★★ Bay of Pigs. A steep wall,

rich in coral and sponges, plunges to depths of over 300m (985 feet).

There are numerous caves to explore and visibility is typically excellent. In many cases, the drop-off is within 90–180m (300–600 feet) offshore. *Hotels Playa Girón and Playa Larga offer diving. See p 78.*

Travel Tip

It's possible to enroll in Open Water diving courses in Cuba. Qualified divers will need their qualification card to dive here. Most dives cost CUC$25–40. Multi-dive offers are generally available. See p 163 for dive tour operators you can book from outside the country.

❼ Santiago de Cuba Prov-

ince. Cuban waters harbor a couple of interesting wrecks. One of the most famous is a Spanish armored cruiser, the 6800-tonne *Cristóbal Colón* destroyed along with the entire Spanish fleet in Santiago Bay on 3 July, 1898, during the Spanish-American war. The dive is usually done from the Brisas Sierra Mar. *See Tour Operators, p 163.*

Dive boat, Maria La Gorda.

Best **Walking**

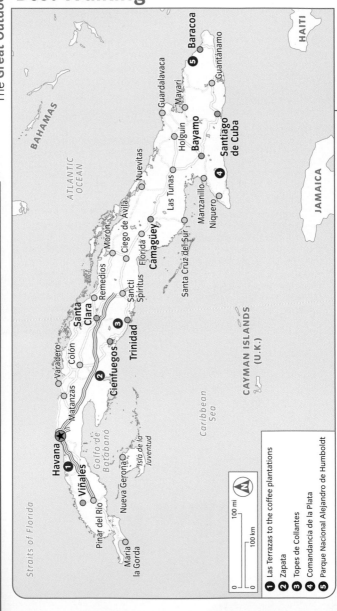

1 Las Terrazas to the coffee plantations
2 Zapata
3 Topes de Collantes
4 Comandancia de la Plata
5 Parque Nacional Alejandro de Humboldt

Most of Cuba's mountainous and walking country is protected by the military (aka the Gaviota Tourist Company). Visitors aren't allowed to wander around rural areas and national parks unaccompanied. Each of the tours in this section can be arranged from well-established starting points where walking guides and appropriate transport can be arranged. The walks here can be off the beaten track and very rewarding, so go slow and enjoy the lush tropical canopy and endemic flora and fauna with the possibility of cooling off at the end in natural pools.

Walk One: ❶ Las Terrazas to the coffee plantations

This 12-km (7½-mile) walk from Las Terrazas leads through lush mountains to abandoned coffee plantations and ends with a dip in the refreshing waters of the San Juan river. The walk itself is moderate but humid, and takes four hours.

This tour starts at **Hotel Moka.** The mountains around Las Terrazas were planted with six million trees in the 1960s to stop erosion. The path through the **UNESCO World Biosphere Reserve,** crosses a river and winds its way through thick, luscious, tangled vegetation. Dozens of epiphytes cling to the trees and

numerous ferns fan out at every turn. Occasional glimpses of views of the mountains—the **Sierra del Rosario**—can be seen. You wander past carob trees, bread trees, coffee plants, rose apples, hibiscus, vanilla orchids, and papyrus plants.

Much of the forest is made up of Cuban pine (*Pinus Caribae*) found only in the Western province of Cuba; Tropical Pine (*Pinus Tropicalis Morelet*), endemic to western Cuba and listed on the IUCN Red List of Threatened Species also grows. You will stop to be shown white pricklyash (*Zanthoxylum martinicense* (Lam.)) known locally as bayua. Watch out not to lean against its

Ruinas de San Ildefonso coffee plantation.

Baños de San Juan.

trunk, which is studded with small conical-shaped thorns. You will also see royal palms, fig, and bamboo.

The forest is alive with rich and delightful pickings for **birdwatchers.** It is likely that you will see or hear the endemic Cuban vireo (*Vireo gundlachii*), yellow-headed warbler (*Teretistris fernandinae*), Cuban emerald hummingbird (*Chlorostilbon ricordii*), Cuban trogon (*Priotelus temnurus*), Cuban tody (*Todus multicolor*) known as the Cartacuba, Cuban green woodpecker (*Xiphidiopicus percussus percussus*), West Indian woodpecker (*Melanerpes superciliaris*),

Cuban peewee (*Contopus caribaeus*), great lizard-cuckoo (*Saurothera merlini*), and stripe-headed tanager (*Spindalis zena*).

San Ildefonso coffee plantation. The French arrived here in 1802 and left in 1862, due to the failure of the local coffee crop. The stone ruins lie buried in vegetation, and you feel as if you've stumbled across them, Indiana Jones-style. The Contento plantation, now also ruined, dates from 1806.

Baños de San Juan. The walk ends with lunch and a well-earned dip in the cascading natural waters of the Baños de San Juan, a series of river pools. *Centro de Visitantes.* ☎ *48/57-8700. www.lasterrazas.cu El Contento walk, CUC$19 including lunch and a dip in the San Juan baths. Reservations can also be made at Hotel Moka (p 69).*

Walk Two: ❷ Zapata
The Zapata Peninsula (p 72) is Cuba's richest bird-watching destination. Eighteen of **Cuba's 21 endemic bird species** can be spotted here, as well as large flocks of resident waterfowl and seasonal migrants. Several trails through and around the national park—Soplillar, Bermejas, and Santo Tomás—are available to birders. At Las Salinas,

Birds of Cuba

Birds that can be spotted on all these walks include the patriotically colored Cuban trogon known as the tocororo. The Cuban national bird, he wears the colors of the Cuban flag — red, white, and blue. He sports a violet blue crown, green back, and deep red lower belly. The voice is distinctive, a to-co-lo-ro call. The Cuban tody is ubiquitous; small and cute, it sports feathers of iridescent green with a bright red throat patch.

Travel to Topes

Although you can rent a car and explore the region on your own, paying a CUC$6.50 entrance fee at the **Topes de Collantes resort** (☎ 42/54-0114; reserva@topes.com.co.cu), hikers are advised to sign on for organized bookings. Many trails are not well marked. The road to Topes is 19km (12 miles) off the main road. There are plenty of curves and some very steep inclines and so confident driving is required. Trinidad agencies also offer excursions.

water birds and flamingoes can be seen. You need a car to drive inland for these excursions.

Set off as early as possible for birdwatching opportunities. The guide will point out the royal palm, wild tamarind (*Lysiloma latisiliquum*), and almácigo (*Bursera simaruba*), known as the tourist tree for its flaking red bark akin to peeling burnt tourists.

On the trip to **Soplillar,** a rare sighting of the Gundlach's hawk (*Gavilán colilargo*), so called for its long tail, may be made from the track. Farther along the mud track, you may see petite Cuban pygmy-owl (*Glaucidium siju siju*) sunning themselves at the top of a tree.

After parking, you walk into the forest. Hurricane Michelle flattened much of the forest here in 2001, and it's currently much harder to spot some species, including the Zunzuncito, bee hummingbird (*Mellisuga helenae*), the world's smallest bird. In the past it was quite common. Here, the Cuban tody flirts on branches and West Indian woodpeckers peck the top of dead palms. The endemic Cuban green woodpecker (*Xiphidiopicus percussus percussus*) is busy pecking; and a Cuban peewee (*Contopus caribaeus*) and a black and orange American redstart (*Setophaga ruticilla*) may make an appearance.

After your birdwatching, you return to the clearing where the car is parked. Here you may spot black smooth-billed ani (*Crotophaga ani*) squawking in low-slung bushes. *You need a permit to enter Zapata Swamp National Park. The park station and entrance (☎ 45/98-7249; pnacionalcz@enet.cu) is located 2km (1¼ miles) north of Playa Larga. The permit costs CUC$10 per person (minimum), and includes a local guide. Orestes Martínez Garcías (El Chino) has more than 30 years experience as an ornithological guide (☎ 45/98-7373; cell: 525 39004; chino.zapata@gmail.com). He charges a minimum of CUC$12 for two hours.*

West Indian woodpecker.

Salto de Caburni.

Walk Three: ❸ Topes de Collantes

Topes de Collantes is a 200-square km (77.2-square mile) area of the Sierra de Escambray that's excellent for hiking. The most popular route is to the Salto del Caburní waterfall. It's a 5-hour excursion and good fitness is required because the return journey is a steep 2km (1¼ mile) ascent.

This hike begins with fresh coffee at the **Casa del Café,** a small museum dedicated to the history of coffee. As you climb by vehicle to the start point don't forget to admire the incredible views of the sea and **Ancón.**

The trail that descends through dense forests of palm, pine, and eucalyptus trees, is fairly challenging, with several **steep descents,** often along a muddy, narrow path. Stop to admire the tall cauliflower-shaped flowers of the yucca, bamboo, dozens of ferns, and the bottlebrush tree (*Callistemon*) with its striking red flowers.

You emerge at a vast exposed **limestone scrape** with views of the luscious forest, dominated by royal palm. Look out for a glimpse of the *tocororo* as well as dozens of species of hummingbird.

Salto del Caburní. This waterfall plunges 75m (246 feet) into a deep green pool. Diving into the swimming hole is most welcome after the walk. Close to the waterfall grows Yamagua (*Guarea trichiloides*); the tea made from the tree delays menstruation for a few days.

Taking Command

You will need to get to Bayamo before heading to the Comandancia de la Plata trail start at Santo Domingo. A national park office (open daily 7.30–10am), sits close to the Hotel Villa Santo Domingo (p 85). You pay a minimum CUC$12 fee to enter the park, which includes a guide. An additional CUC$5 is payable to take pictures of La Comandancia. To gain access, hikers must either climb or take a 4x4 (CUC$5), 15 minutes one-way, or a flatbed truck (CUC$5), 45 minutes one-way; the trip is up a treacherously steep paved road, with thrilling hairpin turns, to Alto de Naranjo, 5km (3 miles) from Santo Domingo.

Humboldt Practicalities

The park is 56km (35 miles) (1¼ hours) from Baracoa along a very bad road. The park office is open from 8am. If you have your own transport you can arrange a tour direct. If not book through Ecotur, C/ Coronel Cardoso 24 (☎ 21/64-3665) or Cubatur, Parque Central (☎ 21/64-5306). Prices range from CUC$5 to CUC$10 per person per trip for those with their own transport. Good boots or sturdy waterproof shoes are required.

Walk Four: ❶ Comandancia de la Plata

Fidel Castro's Revolution HQ during the rebel campaign is buried deep in the **Sierra Maestra,** Cuba's highest and longest mountain range that stretches 140km (87 miles) west to east in the southeast of the country. This historic walk through dense, humid forest takes 1½ hours to reach the rebel command and is fairly easy going. *See also p 32.*

This 6km (4 miles) return hike begins at **Alto de Naranjo.** The rocky trail to La Plata is perched on a mountain ridge. You will pass royal palms, pines, mimosa, and banana plants as clouds float across the trees willow-the-wisp style. The sweet Cartacuba and colorful tocororo (*Priotelus temnurus*) can be seen and heard in the dense vegetation.

After about 20 minutes on the trail, about 800m (2,625 feet) above sea level, is **Alto de Medina.** This small wooden house, at the entrance to base camp, was the checkpoint building. Osvaldo Medina was the first peasant to help Fidel in the mountains.

Farther up along the trail is a small museum. Exhibits reveal the **revolutionary guerrilla warfare** waged in these mountains. A building that was, at one time a small hospital, still stands.

A little farther on are the huts where Fidel lived with his assistant Celia Sánchez. Fidel never allowed anyone but Celia inside the shack; the bench outside the door where he conducted interviews is still there. Ingeniously constructed under the cover of thick forest, the installations make it quite apparent how the rebels eluded capture and assassination.

Peacock at Casa Osvaldo Medina, on the way to Comandancia de la Plata.

Colorful plant, El Recreo trail.

Walk Five: ❺ Parque Nacional Alejandro de Humboldt

Humboldt National Park straddles forest and sea in the far east of Cuba, and is prized for its rich biodiversity and mountainous ecosystem. Within this **UNESCO World Heritage Site** live the world's smallest bat, smallest frog, smallest bird, and smallest male scorpion. There are two trails for visitors and a boat ride around a magnificent protected bay populated by a few manatee.

El Recreo trail. The trail winds slowly 3km (2 miles) into the forest. Walkers start by wandering up a small deep red canyon laden with iron and nickel deposits and emerge into an incongruous woody mix of pine tree and banana plant. Pine cones clutter the path and tiny orchids and pineapple plants trail the curb.

Much of your route is through **flourishing pine forest** (*Pinus Cubensis*); dozens of ferns mat the forest floor. The trail undulates and when the pine needles are down it steadies the path; without the dry covering, the paths would be slippery.

With the highest levels of biodiversity in the West Indies and of unique species in the world, there are numerous plants of interest. Half way along the trail you will see: guao (*Comocladia glabra*), a poisonous plant whose leaves are toxic—human skin becomes inflamed on contact; cereza cimarrona (*Cordia collococea*), a pretty plant with tiny, fuschia-pink baubles; and the El Quiebra Hacha ('axe breaker'), the caguairan (*Hymenaea torrei*). It's an endangered, endemic, extremely hard, deep red wood.

Flowing down from the mountains is the **Río Taco.** Its tepid crystalline waters run over beds of rounded brown pebbles. You will ford the river four times. Close to the end of the trail, you can take a dip, waist-high, in a natural pool.

At the end of the trail return to the park office and take a small boat out into Bahía Taco. Abundant palms and other trees tumble down to the water's edge. The boat will take you down narrow canals between mangrove swamps. Crabs skitter about in the silence. In the cool waters of the bay live a small, elusive group of manatee. ●

Río Taco.

5 The Best **Regional Tours**

Western Cuba

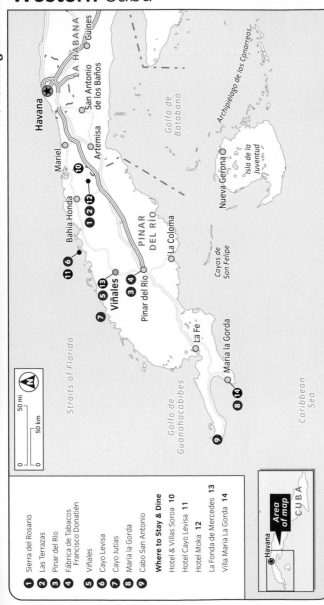

1. Sierra del Rosario
2. Las Terrazas
3. Pinar del Río
4. Fábrica de Tabacos Francisco Donatién
5. Viñales
6. Cayo Levisa
7. Cayo Jutías
8. María la Gorda
9. Cabo San Antonio

Where to Stay & Dine

Hotel & Villas Soroa 10
Hotel Cayo Levisa 11
Hotel Moka 12
La Fonda de Mercedes 13
Villa María La Gorda 14

Western Cuba is a pastoral and underdeveloped region with extraordinary natural beauty. Pinar del Río province is Cuba's prime eco-tourism destination, with excellent rock climbing, mountain biking, hiking, horse-riding, diving, and bird-watching. The hamlet of Viñales is considered one of the most beautiful places in the country. At the island's western tip, María la Gorda is one of Cuba's signature scuba-diving destinations. The province is also Cuba's most heralded tobacco-growing region. START: **Las Terrazas**.

❶ ★ Sierra del Rosario.

Declared a UNESCO biosphere reserve in 1985, the 25,000-hectare (61,776-acre) Sierra del Rosario encompasses a mountainous area of rapidly recovering, secondary tropical deciduous forests, cut with numerous rivers and waterfalls. Nearly 100 species of birds can be spotted, including over half of Cuba's 21 endemic species including the Cuban tody and the bee hummingbird.

Las Terrazas community, Pinar del Río Province.

❷ ★ Las Terrazas. A neat and

organized architectural and social project designed around a working community. The eco-community and Hotel Moka (p 69) are set just above the shores of the diminutive Lago San Juan. There are a half-dozen or so trails and swimming holes, along with a smattering of other attractions, including the Cafetal Buenavista, an abandoned coffee plantation. ☎ *48/57-8555. www.lasterrazas.cu. Daily 9am–6pm. See also p 59.*

Drive 105km (65 miles) south from Las Terrazas to:

❸ Pinar del Río. The provincial

capital is named for the pine trees that grow along the banks of the Río Guamá, where the city is set. Originally founded as Nueva Filipina (New Philippine), it was re-christened Pinar del Río in 1774 and was one of the last major cities founded by the Spanish in Cuba.

❹ Fábrica de Tabacos Francisco Donatién. Several fine

brands of *tabacos* are rolled at this renowned cigar factory. You can walk through the timeless rolling station, where a caller reads news and short stories to keep the rollers interested. The well-stocked Casa del Habano is across the street. *C/ Antonio Maceo, just off Plaza de la Independencia.* ☎ *48/75-3424. Admission CUC$5. Mon–Fri 9am–noon, 1–4pm, Sat 9am–noon.*

Parque Nacional Guanahacabibes, María La Gorda, Pinar del Río Province.

Drive 27km (17 miles) north to:

⑤ ★★★ Viñales. This small, picturesque town is set amid the verdant vegetation, idyllic views, tobacco fields, and *mogote* (limestone) stacks of the Viñales valley. *See p 152.*

Drive 57km (35½ miles) north from Viñales to Palma Rubia, in time for the boat departures.

⑥ ★ Cayo Levisa. The entire northern shore of this little island, only accessible by boat, is one long stretch of white sand fronting a calm and startlingly turquoise sea. The beach is backed alternately by small stands of pine trees and stretches of thick mangrove. There's excellent bird-watching and diving. *Boats depart Palma Rubia at 10am and 6pm returning at 9am and 5pm (30-min journey). CUC$10 return.*

Trips can also be arranged in Viñales.

Drive 52km (32 miles) southwest out of Viñales via La Moncada to Santa Lucia and on to:

⑦ ★ Cayo Jutías. Cayo Jutías is connected to the mainland by an 8-km (5-mile) causeway. Along with a few sunbeds, a restaurant, and nautical center, its highlight is the 8km of deserted white-sand beach and the dozens of enormous orange starfish at Playa Las Estrellas.

Drive 169km (105 miles) south from Viñales via Sandino to:

⑧ ★ María la Gorda. This tiny palm-covered beach and dive resort lies on the eastern end of the long, curving Peninsula de Guanahacabibes. The nearby **Guanahacabibes National Park** has three trails to explore, and you must have a guide to hike any of them. The park ranger station (Estación Ecológica) is at La Bajada. ☎ 48/75-0366. CUC$6–10 per person to hike the trails (starting at 9am). Daily 9am–5pm.

Drive 73km (45 miles) west to Cabo San Antonio. During crab migration in March and April, drive fast over the non-edible crabs so their raised pincers don't puncture your tires.

⑨ Cabo San Antonio. This wild and remote part of Cuba is accessed by a part-tarmacked, part-dust road that runs through lush vegetation and a strange flat outcrop of sharp limestone rocks. The 59-km (36½ miles) road winds its way through crab migration routes, turtle nesting sites, and iguana paths to a lighthouse and the Villa Cabo San Antonio, a set of lonely wooden cabins a short stretch from the sea. This place is for serious divers or nature-lovers only.

Where to **Stay & Dine**

A Note on Hotels & Restaurants

For sleeping and dining options in Viñales, see p 155.

Hotel & Villas Soroa LAS TERRA-ZAS   A stone's throw from the orchid garden in Soroa, the clean and compact rooms at this mini-resort are set around the pool. The best rooms are nos. 16–24, set up stairs leading away from the pool. The pool area becomes a party zone for Cubans at the weekends. *Carretera de Soroa Km 8.* ☎ *48/52-3534. www.hotelescubanacan. com. 49 rooms. CUC$53–65 double w/breakfast. No credit cards. Map p 66.*

★ Hotel Cayo Levisa CAYO LEVISA   If you land one of the oceanfront bungalows in this idyllic little resort, you may never want to leave. The older ones, built in rows parallel to the shore and staggered to guarantee an ocean view, are preferable. ☎ *48/75-6506. www. hotelescubanacan.com. 33 rooms. CUC$67–74 double w/breakfast. No credit cards. Round-trip transportation from Palma Rubia CUC$10. Map p 66.*

★★ Hotel Moka LAS TERRA-ZAS   This is the loveliest rural lodge in Cuba. Each of the bright and spacious rooms has colorful tiled floors and a small balcony. You can also rent small villas, attached to the homes of local residents, on the little lake below the hotel. *Autopista Naciona. Km 51.* ☎ *48/57-8600. www.lasterrazas.cu. 26 rooms, 5 villas. CUC$64–CUC$110 double; CUC$50–CUC$85 villa w/ breakfast. MC, V. Map p 66.*

★ La Fonda de Mercedes LAS TERRAZAS *CRIOLLA*   This is the top dining option in Las Terrazas, even though there are only six items on the menu. The best dish is the Camagüey-style veal, served shredded and cooked in wine, although the grilled chicken a la Pinareña, seasoned with lemon juice and garlic is always tasty. *Edificio 9, Apto. 2, Las Terrazas.* ☎ *48/57-8647. Mains CUC$6.45–8. Lunch & dinner daily.*

Villa María La Gorda MARIA LA GORDA   This place, also known as the International Diving Center, exists somewhere in that gray area between no-frills dive camp and modern resort. The rooms are adequate and fairly spacious, if nothing fancy. If you don't grab one of the older oceanfront units, the huge rustic cabins set back from the beach have a secluded charm. ☎*/fax 48/77-8131. www.gaviota-grupo.com. 55 rooms. CUC$58–68 double w/breakfast. CUC$5 extra for ocean-view room. MC, V. Map p 66.*

Maria La Gorda resort, Pinar del Rio Province.

Central Cuba

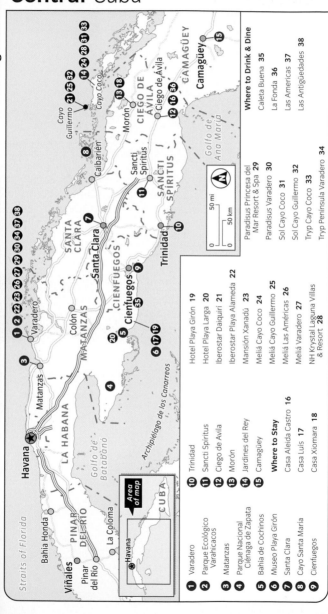

1 Varadero
2 Parque Ecológico Varahicacos
3 Matanzas
4 Parque Nacional Ciénaga de Zapata
5 Bahía de Cochinos
6 Museo Playa Girón
7 Santa Clara
8 Cayo Santa María
9 Cienfuegos
10 Trinidad
11 Sancti Spiritus
12 Ciego de Ávila
13 Morón
14 Jardines del Rey
15 Camagüey

Where to Stay

Casa Aleida Castro 16
Casa Luis 17
Casa Xiomara 18
Hotel Playa Girón 19
Hotel Playa Larga 20
Iberostar Daiquirí 21
Iberostar Playa Alameda 22
Mansión Xanadú 23
Meliá Cayo Coco 24
Meliá Cayo Guillermo 25
Meliá Las Américas 26
Meliá Varadero 27
NH Krystal Laguna Villas & Resort 28
Paradisus Princesa del Mar Resort & Spa 29
Paradisus Varadero 30
Sol Cayo Coco 31
Sol Cayo Guillermo 32
Tryp Cayo Coco 33
Tryp Peninsula Varadero 34

Where to Drink & Dine

Caleta Buena 35
La Fonda 36
Las Américas 37
Las Antiguedades 38

Central Cuba is characterized by a string of historic towns along the spine of the island, and some world-class beaches on the northern coast and preserved wetlands in the south. This is the most visited part of the country and includes Cuba's most famous beach, Varadero, Che Guevara's mausoleum, its little known lapis lazuli-colored waters of the Bay of Pigs, and the beaches of the northern cays. START: **Varadero.**

❶ Varadero. Most of the attractions here lie on or under the sea. Excursions can be arranged through any of Varadero's three marinas or through hotel tour desks. Varadero's highlight, apart from its long golden sands, is the **Mansión Xanadú,** which commands excellent views of the sandy peninsula and the azure Caribbean (p 18). The nicest spot to visit in 'downtown' Varadero is the **Parque Josone,** Av 1 e/ C/ 55 and 58 (☎ 45/66-7228), a beautifully maintained little city park with cool, shady grounds and gardens. There are paths winding around and over little lakes with fountains, several restaurants, and food stands, and the park is dotted with gazebos and park benches. Nearby is the **Museo Municipal Varadero,** C/ 57 and Av de la Playa (☎ 45/61-3189), a blue-and-white wooden building housing an eclectic collection of historic tidbits. *Infotur, C/ 13 esq Av 1.* ☎ *45/ 66-2966; infovar@enet.cu; www .infotur.cu. Parque: daily 9am–11pm. Museo: admission CUC$1; daily 10am–7pm*

❷ Parque Ecológico Varahicacos. A large swathe of the eastern end of the peninsula is protected as the **Varadero Ecological Park.** There are gentle paths through the scrub forests, and you can visit a series of small caves, some of which contain ancient indigenous pictographs. *Admission CUC$3. Daily 9am–4.30pm.*

❸ Matanzas. The 'Athens of Cuba,' on the Bahía de Matanzas, 35km (22 miles) west of Varadero, boasts fine historic buildings and plenty of musical history. *See p 17.*

Mansión Xanadú.

Municipal Museum, Varadero.

Drive southwest to the Autopista from Matanzas and then east to Jagüey Grande where a café marks the entrance road to the Zapata peninsula that juts off the southern coast of Matanzas province.

❹ ★ Parque Nacional Ciénaga de Zapata. The Zapata peninsula itself is almost entirely uninhabited; most of it is protected as part of the **Zapata Swamp National Park,** a haven for bird-watchers and naturalists. You need a permit to enter the park. The park station and entrance (☎ 45/98-7249) is located 2km (1¼ miles) north of **Playa Larga.** *See p 60.*

❺ Bahía de Cochinos. The eastern edge of the Zapata coastline is defined by the **Bay of Pigs,** the site of the failed 1961 US-backed invasion of Cuba (p 78). The Bay of Pigs, and **Playa Girón** in particular, is a kind of national shrine to this stunning David-over-Goliath victory. Just off the shore, all along the Bay and toward the east, the coast drops off steeply for 305km (1,000 feet) or more, making this a true haven for scuba divers.

Travel Tip

Bring plenty of mosquito repellent to Zapata. This is an area of vast

Palm Tree Paradise

At 108m (360 feet), the Bacuanayagua Bridge is the highest in Cuba. It spans the Yumuri Valley that rolls with millions of royal palms. Most tourist buses stop here for a quick break and photo opportunity, and if you're driving, you'll want to do the same. A rugged side road leads off the highway if you want to explore this largely undeveloped valley. It's untainted by tourism and provides a window into a rural world little changed in a hundred years. The bridge is 7km (4 miles) west of Matanzas, on the Vía Blanca en route from Havana to Matanzas and Varadero.

swampland, and so mosquitoes can be fierce, particularly if there's no wind.

6 Museo Playa Girón. Two rooms inside this simple little museum contain a series of photos, relics, and a written history detailing the Bay of Pigs invasion and battles, as well as other local history. A 15-minute documentary video (in Spanish) is shown throughout the day, and outside you can see the wreckage of tanks, heavy artillery, and a downed US plane. The written explanations are in Spanish only. ☎ 45/98-4122. Admission CUC$2. Additional CUC$1 for a guide. CUC$1 to see the documentary. CUC$1 to take photos. Daily 8am–5pm.

From Jagüey Grande drive 128km (80 miles) east along the Autopista to Santa Clara, 6km (4 miles) off the highway.

7 ★ Santa Clara. This medium-sized university city is home to Che Guevara's mausoleum. See p 138.

8 ★★★ Cayo Santa María. If more beaches appeal, this recently developed resort offers seclusion and a more exclusive air, in parts, than Varadero, although at its top end an enormous hotel city is under construction. The beaches are an undisturbed brilliant white sloping into an aquamarine sea.

From Santa Clara drive 12km (7½ miles) west to the junction with Ranchuelo. Take the secondary road 48km (30 miles)

south through the attractive town of Palmira to:

9 ★ Cienfuegos. A French-influenced port city with a small attractive center dominated by historic buildings. See p 124.

From Cienfuegos, drive east and south to take the scenic coastal road east, some 81km (50½ miles), to:

10 ★★★ Trinidad. This is an exquisitely preserved Spanish colonial town. See p 146.

From Trinidad, take the road northeast, 70km (43½ miles), to:

11 Sancti Spíritus. One of the original villas founded in Cuba, Sancti Spíritus is a small, sleepy Spanish colonial town with a handful of outstanding buildings. See p 134.

Drive 76km (47 miles) east along the main highway to:

12 Ciego de Avila. This pleasant colonial town is known as the city of portales for its multiple and multi-colored columns.

Drive 37km (23 miles) north of Ciego de Avila to:

13 Morón. This small town is the gateway to the most developed northern coast cays in Cuba and home to most of the 3,500 Cubans who work at the resort hotels. With just a few dusty streets traveled by bicycles, horse-drawn carriages, and the rare antique American auto, charmingly low-key Morón is most notable for its splendid but dilapidated collection of colonial buildings that line the main street, Calle Martí. Most travelers are content to stroll up and down

Che monument, Santa Clara.

The Sugar Supremacy

You pass many tall chimney stacks surrounded by creaking industrial architecture while driving through Central Cuba. These are the abandoned sugar factories that powered Cuba for years. On his second voyage to the West Indies, Christopher Columbus brought the sugar plant from the Canaries. Conditions were ripe for exploitation in Cuba. In the 18th and 19th century the steam train powered the sugar revolution, aided by millions of African slaves. Cuba became a mono cropping producer: at its export height, the country was the world's fourth largest producer of the sweet stuff. At the **Museo de Agroindustria Azucarero Marcelo Salado** (☎ 42/36-3286), north of Remedios, you can visit this decommissioned factory founded in 1891. Interesting models and exhibits explain the beginnings from the use of oxen revolving around a mill to factory monolith. Open Mondays to Fridays and alternate Saturdays 7am–4pm. Admission CUC$3. A restored steam train makes a journey to Remedios for CUC$9, if there are enough visitors.

Martí, soaking up the relaxed local flavor. The town mascot is the cock of Morón, a bronze statue placed at the foot of a clock tower near the Hotel Morón (the cock crows twice daily).

Drive 56km (35 miles) north of Morón to Cayo Coco. Cayo Guillermo is a farther 31km (19 miles) to the west on a tarmacked road. Pass a checkpoint (passports required) before driving across the 27-km (17 miles) causeway (toll: CUC$2 each way) to the cays known collectively as:

⓮ ★★ **Jardines del Rey.** With long, pristine stretches of coral reef, and warm, crystal-clear waters, the cays are one of the best diving spots on the island. One of the finest beaches in Cuba is **Playa Pilar,** with its golden sands and perfect blue seas lapping at the shore. Ernest Hemingway used to fish here (p 34). The cays are also famous for flamingos, and flamingo tours, from hotels, are possible.

Return to Ciego de Avila and drive 108km (67 miles) along the Autopista to:

⓯ ★★ **Camagüey.** The historic center of this city of churches was anointed as a UNESCO World Heritage Site in 2008. See p 120.

Cayo Guillermo, Jardines del Rey.

Where to **Stay**

Central Cuba Accommodation

For accommodation in Matanzas, see p 131; for Santa Clara, p 139; for Cienfuegos, p 127; for Trinidad, p 150; for Sancti Spiritus, p 135, and for Camagüey, p 122.

Casa Aleida Castro CIEGO DE AVILA A smart maroon-painted 1959 modern house with oriental accents. The original bathrooms are still in place, and the top floor room opens out on to a huge terrace. The owners used to run a *paladar* (a restaurant in their home) and so the evening meal is always delicious and plentiful. *C/ 3 No 6 e/ Independencia and Joaquín de Agüero.* ☎ *33/22-8355. CUC$25 double w/o breakfast. No credit cards. Map p 70.*

Casa Luís PLAYA GIRON This modern home, with two air-conditioned, comfortable rooms and a large patio, is one of the most hospitable in Cuba. Luís and his family are friendly and go out of their way to assist with any of their guests' needs. It also has secure parking and is close to the beach. *Carretera a Cienfuegos esq Carretera a Playa Larga (marked by lion-topped columns).* ☎ *45/98-4258. Two rooms. CUC$20–25 double w/breakfast. No credit cards. Map p 70.*

Casa Xiomara MORÓN The welcome at this modern, modest family home in Morón is one of the best in Cuba. Lisbeth and her family are eager to help. She also works on the cays and so can offer tourist advice. The air-conditioned room is in a small, independent *casita* with an en suite bathroom. Relax in the rocking chairs outside under huge hibiscus flowers. *C/ 8 no. 2-C, e/ C/*

Sordo y C. ☎ *33/50-4236. ysary@ trocha.cav.sld.cu. One room. CUC$20 double w/o breakfast. No credit cards. Map p 70.*

Hotel Playa Girón PLAYA GIRON Recent remodeling has greatly improved the furnishings and decor at this series of ranch bungalows. The beach is acceptable and the water is lovely, but the view is obscured by an ugly breakwater. This is really only for hard-core divers or bird-watchers. ☎ *45/98-4110. www.hoteles cubanacan.com. 133 rooms. CUC$52–66 double all-inclusive. MC, V. Map p 70.*

Hotel Playa Larga PLAYA LARGA The complex here is undergoing refurbishment. New rooms are compact and come with modern furnishings; some of the *casitas* are spacious with two bedrooms and a small sitting area attached. The small patch of beach here is acceptable, but the place is best for serious divers and bird-watchers. *Playa Larga.* ☎ *45/98-7294. www. hotel escubanacan.com. 68 rooms.*

Casa Luís, Playa Girón.

Hotel Playa Larga.

CUC$54–66 double w/breakfast. MC, V. Map p 70.

★★ Iberostar Daiquirí CAYO GUILLERMO

Three-story blocks on a beautiful section of beach sit around a large pool surrounded by gardens, with a host of smaller buildings spread around ample grounds. The better rooms have views of the ocean. ☎ *33/30-1650. www. iberostar.com. 312 rooms. CUC$167–560 double all-inclusive. MC, V. Map p 70.*

★★★ kids Iberostar Playa Alameda PUNTA HICACOS

An attractively designed resort, the rooms here are housed in a series of three-story units spread around the resort's expansive grounds. A broad pedestrian-only avenue leads from the reception to the large complex of pools, which includes a well-designed children's play area. *Las Morlas Km 15.* ☎ *45/66-8822. www. iberostar.com. 391 rooms. CUC$219–577 double all-inclusive. MC, V.*

★ Mansión Xanadú CENTRAL VARADERO

The former mansion of Irénée Dupont de Nemours is now a hotel. Although this is certainly the most distinctive boutique hotel in Varadero, its 1930s grandeur feels a little dated. However, the rooms are all spacious and meticulously maintained, with sparkling marble floors and antique furnishings. Most have narrow, intricately carved wooden balconies overlooking the ocean. Guests can use the neighboring Meliá Las Américas facilities. *Carretera Las Américas Km 8.5.* ☎ *45/66-8482. www.varaderogolfclub.com. Six rooms. CUC$150–210 double w/ breakfast. MC, V. Map p 70.*

★★★ Meliá Cayo Coco CAYO COCO

This elegant Meliá flagship is the top hotel on Cayo Coco. The property is hip and stylish throughout; chic for a beach-based all-inclusive break. The resort has 76 bungalow rooms built out over a natural lagoon. First floor rooms have private balconies close to the lapping water. The hotel's excellent stretch of beach, Playa Las Coloradas, fronts a pretty, protected bay. ☎ *33/30-1180. www.solmeliacuba. com. 250 rooms. CUC$190–380 double all-inclusive. Children under 18 not allowed. MC, V. Map p 70.*

★★ kids Meliá Cayo Guillermo CAYO GUILLERMO

The fanciest property on Cayo Guillermo, this hotel wraps around an extensive pool area. Its swathe of beach is one of the finest on the cays, with thick palm trees sprouting out of pristine white sand. Low-key hotel blocks feature large, bright, and comfortable rooms, but the buffet restaurant isn't up to scratch. ☎ *33/30-1680. www.solmeliacuba. com. 301 rooms. CUC$168–267 double all-inclusive. MC, V. Map p 70.*

Meliá Las Américas CENTRAL VARADERO

Located just by the clubhouse and first tee of Cuba's only 18-hole golf course, this upscale hotel is the golfer's top choice. The rooms are spread among lush gardens amid a maze of swimming pools and ponds. The hotel sits right on a small section of beautiful beach. *Autopista del Sur, Carretera Las Morlas.* 📞 *45/66-7600. www.solmeliacuba.com. 290 rooms. CUC$179–482 double all-inclusive. MC, V. Children under 18 not allowed. Map p 70.*

★★ **Meliá Varadero** CENTRAL VARADERO   This large hotel sits on a rocky outcrop with small sections of fine beach on either side. Seven pyramid-like spokes extend off a massive and lush central atrium lobby. Rooms are large, contemporary, and comfortable. Almost all the rooms have some view of the water; the farther out on each spoke, the better the view. *Autopista del Sur Km 7, Carretera Las Morlas.* 📞 *45/66-7013. www.melia-varadero.com. 490 rooms. CUC$176–450 double all-inclusive. MC, V. Map p 70.*

★★ **NH Krystal Laguna Villas & Resort** CAYO COCO   Half the rooms at this hotel, which features outstanding facilities, are corporate-style blocks, while the others are attractive, wooden cabin-like *casitas* built over a natural lagoon. The latter come with living rooms and balconies. The beach, hidden behind the lagoon, isn't visible from the property. 📞 *33/30-1470. www.nh-hotels.com. 690 rooms. CUC$130–190 double all-inclusive. MC, V. Map p 70.*

★★ **Paradisus Princesa del Mar Resort & Spa** PUNTA HICACOS   The rooms, facilities, and grounds here are all quite grand. There's a sort of modern plantation styling throughout and white parasols and gazebos with wafting curtains surrounding the pool. The hotel rooms are attractive with handsome linens, and can all be considered junior suites, at the very least. *Autopista del Sur, Carretera Las Morlas.* 📞 *45/66-7200. www.solmeliacuba.com. 434 rooms. CUC$292–561 double all-inclusive. Children under 18 not allowed. MC, V. Map p 70.*

★★★ **Paradisus Varadero** PUNTA RINCON FRANCES   Set at the eastern end of the peninsula on a remote section of beach, this is the Sol Meliá chain's fanciest hotel in Varadero. Most rooms here are large junior suites with sunken sitting rooms that let out onto either a private terrace or balcony. Only a small percentage of rooms have an ocean view. *Autopista del Sur Km 15.*

Hotel Meliá Cayo Guillermo, Jardines del Rey.

The Bay of Pigs

On 16th April, 1961, a force of 1,400 Cuban exiles, backed by the United States, landed at several beach points along the Bay of Pigs in an ill-fated attempt to overthrow Fidel Castro. They were met by Cuban forces, led by Castro, and quickly defeated. Fighting lasted less than 72 hours. Though they were trained and supported—and even escorted—by the US military and CIA, the invaders were left to fight on their own (President Kennedy was reluctant to commit direct US forces). The lack of air support and serious tactical blunders also contributed to the rout. The battle took the lives of 160 Cubans and around 120 mercenary fighters. Some 1,195 of the invading troops were captured, most released 20 months later in an exchange with the US for food, medical supplies, and hospital equipment. Today, the Bay of Pigs remains a source of pride to Cuba's government, and a bitter pill for anti-Castro opponents.

☎ 45/66-8700. www.solmeliacuba. com. 421 rooms. CUC$292–561 double all-inclusive. MC, V. Map p 70.

★ kids **Sol Cayo Coco** CAYO COCO   This is the best-suited hotel on the cay for families. The kids' club, minigolf, soccer field, and kid's corner restaurant are tailored to youngsters. It's the only hotel with two beaches—it sits on a nice expanse of Playa Las Coloradas and also offers guests access to a sensational, secluded section of Playa Larga. The hotel underwent a major upgrade in 2009. ☎ 33/30-1280. www.solmeliacuba.com. 270 rooms. CUC$155-166 double all-inclusive. MC, V. Map p 70.

★★ kids **Sol Cayo Guillermo** CAYO GUILLERMO   This well-designed hotel, refurbished in 2008, has a relaxed vibe. Rooms are bright and cheery. The best are the bungalows set close to the white sandy beach, although the second floor superior rooms with large private balconies are also a good bet. ☎ 33/30-1760. www.solmeliacuba. com. 490 rooms. CUC$124–248 double all-inclusive. MC, V. Map p 70.

★★ **Tryp Cayo Coco** CAYO COCO   The granddaddy of all the Cayo hotels, this resort has refurbished smart, cheery rooms, with open-air balconies. Many of the rooms have sea views. The pool areas are ample, with lots of greenery. Unfortunately, much of the property is exposed and surrounded by unsympathetic architecture, and so it isn't as intimate as the Meliá Cayo Coco. ☎ 33/30-1300. www.solmelia.com. 508 rooms. CUC$135–267 double all-inclusive. MC, V. Map p 70.

★★★ kids **Tryp Peninsula Varadero** PUNTA HICACOS   The facilities are top-notch here and the children's area a standout, with a large children's pool that's a virtual amusement park. The rooms are housed in a series of attractive three-story Key West-style buildings. Located toward the far eastern end of the peninsula, the hotel is on a beautiful stretch of beach. *Autopista del Sur Km 17.5.* ☎ 45/66-8800. www.solmeliacuba.com. 591 rooms. CUC$206–479 double all-inclusive. MC, V. Map p 70.

Where to **Drink & Dine**

A Note on Drinking & Dining

For dining options in Matanzas, see p 131; for Santa Clara, p 139; for Cienfuegos, p 127; for Trinidad, p 150; for Sancti Spíritus, p 135; and for Camagüey, p 122.

kids Caleta Buena PLAYA GIRON *SEAFOOD* This seaside grill serves up platters of lobster, fish, and crocodile and, for the price, a flan and coffee is included as well as an open bar. *Carretera Caleta Buena, 8km (5 miles) from Playa Girón. No phone. CUC\$15. No credit cards. Lunch daily (open 10am–5pm).*

La Fonda CIEGO DE AVILA *CRIOLLA* A sweet restaurant housed in an attractive blue colonial building with a rustic flair offering some bargain *menu del días* (set daily menus) of five dishes. Opt for the shrimps in garlic, fried chicken, or the house specialty, *ropa vieja* (shredded steak in a tomato sauce base). Dine

outside under the *portales*. *C/ Maximo Gomez esq C/ Honorato Castillo. ☎ 33/26-6186. Mains CUC\$1.50–5.50. No credit cards. Lunch & dinner daily.*

★ **Las Americas** VARADERO *INTERNATIONAL* The best seats are those on the ocean-front veranda of the Mansión Xanadú, at wooden tables set with heavy china. Here at the most elegant restaurant in town, the food is old-school French and Continental, adequately done but no better. *Carretera Las Américas Km 8.5. ☎ 45/66-7388. Mains CUC\$12–45. MC, V. Lunch & dinner daily; reservations essential.*

★ **Las Antigüedades** VARADERO *CRIOLLA* Religious statues, enormous vases, and glass chandeliers grace this popular restaurant. Dine on grilled lobster or *criolla* (traditional Cuban) cuisine and soak up the atmosphere. *Av. 1 and C/ 59. ☎ 45/66-7329. Mains CUC\$11–25. MC, V. Lunch & dinner daily.*

Caleta Buena restaurant, Playa Girón.

Oriente

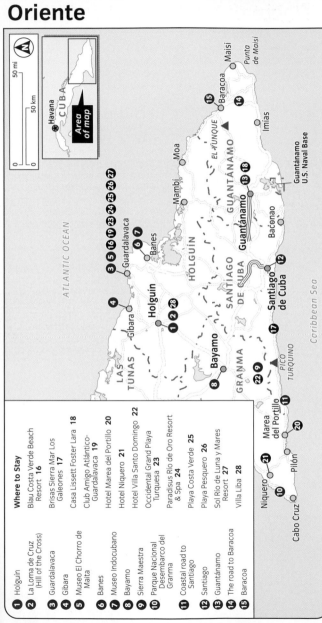

1 Holguín
2 La Loma de Cruz (Hill of the Cross)
3 Guardalavaca
4 Gibara
5 Museo El Chorro de Maíta
6 Banes
7 Museo Indocubano
8 Bayamo
9 Sierra Maestra
10 Parque Nacional Desembarco del Granma
11 Coastal road to Santiago
12 Santiago
13 Guantánamo
14 The road to Baracoa
15 Baracoa

Where to Stay

Blau Costa Verde Beach Resort **16**
Brisas Sierra Mar Los Galeones **17**
Casa Lissett Foster Lara **18**
Club Amigo Atlántico-Guardalavaca **19**
Hotel Marea del Portillo **20**
Hotel Niquero **21**
Hotel Villa Santo Domingo **22**
Occidental Grand Playa Turquesa **23**
Paradisus Río de Oro Resort & Spa **24**
Playa Costa Verde **25**
Playa Pesquero **26**
Sol Río de Luna y Mares Resort **27**
Villa Liba **28**

The hot and steamy Oriente is where you find the southern swathe of the **Sierra Maestra,** dramatic coastlines, and a collection of historic cities and the northern beach resort of Guadalavaca. Along the southern coast of the province, a bad road backed by wild scenery brings you to Santiago de Cuba, the island's second city. Known as the Cradle of the Revolution, it was where Fidel Castro claimed victory in 1959. START: Holguín.

❶ Holguín. The provincial capital, officially called **San Isidoro de Holguín,** is a pleasant but unremarkable place. **Parque Calixto García,** named for a 19th-century patriot, represents the heart of the city.

❷ La Loma de Cruz (Hill of the Cross). Some 3km (2 miles) north of Holguin, this peak can be climbed by ascending the nearly 500 steps to the top, where there's a wooden cross erected in 1790. From the summit you can see the entire city spread out below.

Drive 57km (35½ miles) northeast of Holguín along an upgraded tarmacked road to the beach resorts collectively known as:

❸ Guardalavaca. The spectacular beaches tracing the coast are more than 1,200km (750 miles) of pure white beaches lined by royal palm trees, framed by exuberant vegetation and fronting some of the clearest, most inviting waters of Cuba. The best beaches are **Esmeralda, Pesquero, Yuraguanal,** and **Guardalavaca**—all of which have major hotels lining them. Horseback riding, as well as all watersports and excursions, are popular.

Playa Guardalavaca.

Travel Tip

In May and early June, Guardalavaca is wet with heavy tropical rains. August is sweltering and too humid for all but the most devoted sun worshippers.

From Guardalavaca, drive 23km (14 miles) south to Santa Lucía and then west along a bad road to Floro Pérez for 42km (26 miles) before heading north 17km (11 miles) to:

❹ ★ Gibara. This sleepy, charming, early-19th-century provincial port— sometimes referred to as La Villa Blanca (White Village) due to its one-time whitewashed appearance—is home to a number of fine colonial-style buildings. Gibara is a modest fishing town with great scenery that overlooks a wide natural bay, with a very tranquil atmosphere.

Return to Guardalavaca, drive a couple of kilometers southeast to Yaguajay.

❺ ★ Museo El Chorro de Maita. This collection represents the largest and most important discovery of a Native American cemetery in Cuba; the community dates

View from the southern coastal road.

from 1490–1540. The burial ground contains the well-preserved remains of 108 Taíno people including a single Spaniard, most likely a friar, whose body is marked by a cross. Many other burial objects are displayed in cases. *Cerro de Yaguajay, near Guardalavaca.* ☎ *24/43-0201. Admission CUC$2. Daily 9am–5pm.*

From Guardalavaca, drive 34km (21 miles) southeast to:

⑥ Banes. A slow-moving, dusty little town, Banes is best known for its unlikely association with the towering figures of 20th-century Cuba. Fulgencio Batista, whose government the Castro rebels deposed in 1959, was born here in 1901. Fidel Castro and his brother, Raúl, were born nearby in **Birán**.

Castro's landing route, Parque Nacional Desembarco del Granma.

⑦ ★ Museo Indocubano. This Banes museum boasts a pre-Columbian collection of 20,000 or so exhibits of ceramics, jewelry, tools, and a valuable 13th-century gold 'idol of Banesa,' just 4cm (1½ inches) high. *Av. General Marreo 305, Banes.* ☎ *24/48-2487. Admission CUC$1. Tues–Sat 9am–5pm, Sun 8am–noon.*

Return to Guardalavaca and Holguín before heading an easy 71km (44 miles) on good roads south to:

⑧ Bayamo. Cuba's second city founded by the Spaniards is today a sleepy town with little tourism. *See p 116.*

⑨ ★ Sierra Maestra. The Sierra Maestra is a mountainous region tumbling down to the southern coast, with a well-known place in the recent history of Cuba. *See p 32 and p 118.*

Drive east to Manzanillo and then south to Niquero and beyond.

⑩ Parque Nacional Desembarco del Granma. Walk through the mangroves along a concrete path to visit the actual spot where the Castro rebels disembarked. Follow this with a visit to the small museum and house where the first peasant to shelter the rebels, Angel Perez Rosabal, lived. South of the park, the El Guafe trails take you through a jagged limestone landscape peppered with cactus and alive with birds. Caves feature ancient carved idols. South of El Guafe is the Cabo Cruz lighthouse and fishing village. *Playa Las Coloradas, 13km (8 miles) south of Niquero. Admission CUC$5. Daily 7am–6pm.*

Return to Niquero and drive southeast to Pilón for the:

⓫ ★★ Coastal road to Santiago. The Sierra Maestra stretching down to the rocky beaches and black sands of the south coast, set against the sparkling blue waters of the Caribbean, is one of the most dramatic sights in Cuba. The road is remarkably absent of villages for long stretches. The beaches, such as they are, range from soft gray stone to forbidding big black rock. A smattering of resorts are located at points along the coast. The road isn't consistently in good condition and there are broken bridges. Gravel tracks have been forged around the bridges but advance warning isn't always available. Journey takes around 7 hours driving at 40kph (25mph). Always check first whether the road is passable, in Santiago or Pilón.

⓬ Santiago. Cuba's hot and lively second city. *See p 140.*

Drive north and then east 84km (52 miles) to:

⓭ Guantánamo. Near this pleasant, quiet provincial city is the infamous US military base of **Guantánamo Bay.** Gitmo has about 3,000 full-time residents who, although surrounded on three sides by Cuba, live as if they are in American 'suburbotopia,' with typical suburban homes and US goods.

Drive 150km (93 miles) east to Baracoa, skirting Guantánamo Bay.

⓮ ★★★ The road to Baracoa. The parched cactus-dominated landscape of the southern coast begins to change gradually in color along the spectacular 40-km (25-mile) road, La Farola, which winds its way through the mountains to Baracoa. Things get ever more lush, with thick tropical vegetation and views at every turn.

⓯ Baracoa. The colonial town of Baracoa, isolated from the rest of Cuba before the building of the road, is a beguiling little place, known for its chocolate and coconut and connections to Columbus. It's been known to bewitch more than a few travelers into staying much longer than they planned. *See p 112.*

Guantánamo town center.

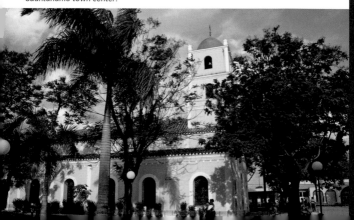

The Best Regional Tours

Where to **Stay**

Travel Tip

For dining options in Bayamo, Santiago, and Baracoa, see p 118, p 144, and p 115 respectively.

★★ kids Blau Costa Verde Beach Resort PLAYA PESQUERO

This resort consists of big building blocks painted in blinding bright orange and blue, with three open-air restaurants built around a large figure-eight pool. Rooms are cheery and the sands are just a 50-m walk away. The beach is lovely, and the water has amazing crystal-clear turquoise tones. ☎ 24/43-3510. www.blau-hotels.com. 309 rooms. CUC$108–163 double all-inclusive. MC, V. Map p 80.

★ Brisas Sierra Mar Los Galeones CHIVIRICO

A multi-tiered hotel overlooking a fine, black sand beach. The overall facilities are impressive—six restaurants, three bars, two tennis courts, a fitness room, and a large swimming pool—but the rooms are fairly standard. The Galeones hotel—a separate property perched on a steep hill—clusters around a small pool and enjoys wonderful views of the sea and Sierra Maestra. Sierra Mar: Carretera a Chivirico, Km 60. ☎ 22/32-9110. www.hotelescubanacan.com. 200 rooms. CUC$70–138 double all-inclusive. Los Galeones: ☎ 22/32-6160. 34 rooms. CUC$78–118 double all-inclusive. MC, V. Map p 80.

Casa Lissett Foster Lara GUANTANAMO

An enormous second-floor apartment with two large dining rooms. One room is off the dining area with attractive, preserved art-deco furniture while the second is upstairs and opens out onto the roof terrace with a semi-independent entrance. Lissett is a very friendly casa owner and speaks good English. C/ Pedro A Pérez 761 e/ Jesús del Sol y Prado. ☎ 21/32-5790. Two rooms. CUC$15–20 double w/o breakfast. No credit cards. Map p 80.

Club Amigo Atlántico-Guardalavaca GUARDALAVACA

This fusion of several resorts, three large, 1970s Soviet-style blocks

Hotel Los Galeones, part of Brisas Sierra Mar Los Galeones, Chivirico.

situated around an old pool, is Guardalavaca's budget option. However, the newer villas are considerably nicer and closer to the beach. The hotel has only a tiny cove beach, with the main beach a considerable walk. ☎ *24/43-0180. www.hoteles cubanacan.com. 747 rooms. 144 villas. CUC$50–164 double all-inclusive. MC, V. Map p 80.*

Hotel Marea del Portillo PILON
This pleasant low-rise all-inclusive hotel on the southern coast near Pilón sits on an attractive curve of black sand beach. This is the only place to stay on the western stretch of the spectacular south coast road (p 83, ⑪). ☎ *23/59-7081. www. hotelescubanacan.com. 283 rooms. CUC$60–130 double all inclusive. MC, V. Map p 80.*

Hotel Niquero NIQUERO   A small modern hotel in the center of this pleasant town that serves tourists visiting the Granma park (p 82, ⑩). Rooms are adequate and comfortable; service is with a smile, but food on the menu isn't always available. *C/ Marti 100 e/ Céspedes and 2 de Diciembre.* ☎ *59-2367. 26 rooms. CUC$18 double w/breakfast. No credit cards. Map p 80.*

Hotel Villa Santo Domingo
SANTO DOMINGO   These 20 attractive little en suite cabins, nestled on the banks of the River Yara, come equipped with twin beds, air conditioning, TVs, solar-powered hot water, and refrigerators. Also in the grounds are a good restaurant, La Yamagua, and an outdoor grill. This is the closest hotel to the Commandancia La Plata del Ejército Rebelde. ☎ *23/56-5568. www.islazul.cu. 20 rooms. CUC$34–37 double w/ breakfast. No credit cards. Map p 80.*

★★ **kids** **Occidental Grand Playa Turquesa** PLAYA YURAGUA-NAL   This large, fairly anonymous

Beach by the Hotel Marea del Portillo, Pilón.

and spread-out resort, set above a broad beach and next to natural forests, boasts seven swimming pools. There are several good à la carte dining options, as well as the ubiquitous large buffets. The hotel offers an extensive array of watersports, activities, and a children's program. ☎ *24/43-3540. www.occidental hotels.com. 500 rooms. CUC$209–238 double all-inclusive. MC, V. Map p 80.*

★★★ **Paradisus Río de Oro Resort & Spa** PLAYA ESMERALDA
One of the most luxurious all-inclusive resorts in Cuba, this Meliá flagship hotel is perched above a low, rocky cliff overlooking the beach. Handsome, two-story room blocks are set amid lush, landscaped gardens. The superb main beach is a short walk down some stairs built into the cliff. This property also benefits from a series of semi-private coves. ☎ *24/43-0090. www.sol meliacuba.com. 300 rooms. CUC$258–CUC$291 double, all-inclusive. MC, V. Children under 18 not allowed. Map p 80.*

Dismal Dining

Cuba isn't known for its dining scene. The majority of food for tourists is imported and the state runs all restaurants, which are largely found only in areas of tourist development. Small concessions to private enterprise are *paladares*. Cuba permitted limited private enterprise in the mid-1990s after the Soviet Union withdrew aid and subsidies: *paladares* are restaurants set up in private Cuban homes. Legally they can only offer 12 seats, can't serve shrimp or lobster, and are heavily taxed by the state. However, the best food in the country is served in these small oases of creative cuisine. All hotels feature restaurants and nearly all *casas particulares* (private rented rooms) offer dinner.

★★ **kids** **Playa Costa Verde**
PLAYA PESQUERO   This resort is excellent value for families. Although rooms don't have sea or beach views, they represent some of the best-equipped and best-designed rooms among high-end beach hotels in Cuba. The hotel offers a wide range of activities and an excellent children's program. A spectacular section of Playa Pesquero is a five-minute walk from the pool. ☎ *24/43-3520. www.gaviota-grupo.com. 480 rooms. CUC$80–115 double all-inclusive. MC, V. Map p 80.*

★★ **Playa Pesquero** PLAYA PESQUERO   This massive hotel has spacious and cheery rooms, all in two-story blocks spread around the enormous grounds ringing the large free-form pool, spa, and entertainment area. At the very least, staying here would give you a good workout: you can barely even glimpse the sleeping blocks from the central pool area. ☎ *24/43-3530. www.gaviota-grupo.com. 912 rooms. CUC$200–280 double all-inclusive. MC, V. Map p 80.*

★★ **kids** **Sol Río de Luna y Mares Resort** PLAYA ESMERALDA   These two modern Sol Meliá properties are joined at the hip. The Río de Luna is more attractive with a medium-size pool; the feel of the hotel is more intimate. The Río de Mares, though somewhat newer, has a slightly more impersonal atmosphere. The range of activities and facilities, and a well-run children's program, make this an excellent choice for families. ☎ *24/43-0060. www.solmeliacuba.com. 464 rooms. CUC$167–269 double all-inclusive. MC, V. Map p 80.*

Villa Liba HOLGUIN   Run by Jorge Mezerene, this is one marvelous 1950s mansion. This listed modern home has two spacious rooms close to an interior patio, an interesting quirk. There's original 1950s furniture, Jorge's cooking with natural ingredients, and interest in the environment to win you over. *C/ Maceo 46 esq C/ 18. ☎ 24-423823. Two rooms. CUC$25 double w/o breakfast. No credit cards. Map p 80.* ●

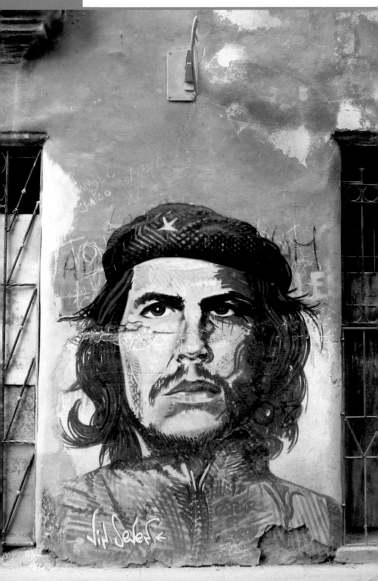

Havana

1. Plaza de Armas
2. El Templete
3. Castillo de la Real Fuerza
4. Museo de la Ciudad
5. Café O'Reilly
6. Catedral de San Cristóbal
7. Mercado Tacón
8. Centro Wifredo Lam
9. Cafetería El Portal
10. Plaza Vieja
11. Plaza de San Francisco
12. Calle Obispo
13. Museo Nacional de Bellas Artes
14. Museo de Arte Universal
15. Café La Barrita
16. Museo de la Revolución y Memorial Granma
17. El Malecón
18. Parque Central
19. Prado
20. El Capitolio
21. Fábrica de Tabaco Partagás
22. Parque Histórico Morro y Cabaña (Castillo del Morro)
23. Parque Histórico Morro y Cabaña (La Fortaleza de San Carlos de la Cabaña)

Where to Stay

Casa Eduardo Canciano 24
Casa Evora Rodríguez 25
Casa Federico y Yamelis Llanes 26
Casa Mary 27
Casa Melba and Alberto 28
Chez Nous 29
Hotel Ambos Mundos 30
Hotel Conde de Villanueva 31
Hotel del Tejadillo 32
Hotel Florida 33
Hotel Inglaterra 34
Hotel Los Frailes 35
Hotel Plaza 36
Hotel Raquel 37

Hotel Santa Isabel 38
Hotel Saratoga 39
Hotel Sevilla 40
Hotel Telégrafo 41
La Casona de Obrapia 42
NH Parque Central 43
Park View Hotel 44

Where to Drink & Dine

Café del Oriente 45
Cafetería El Portal 46
El Templete 47

La Dominica 48
La Taberna de la Muralla 49
Los Nardos 50
Roof Garden Restaurant 51
Santo Angel 52

Nightlife, Arts & Entertainment

Casa de la Música Centro Habana 53
Cuban National Ballet 54
Lluvia de Oro 55

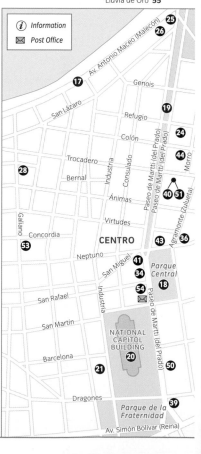

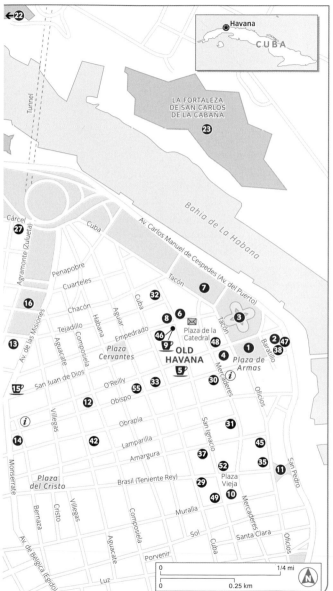

Havana

CUBA

LA FORTALEZA
DE SAN CARLOS
DE LA CABAÑA

Bahía de La Habana

Vedado & **Playa**

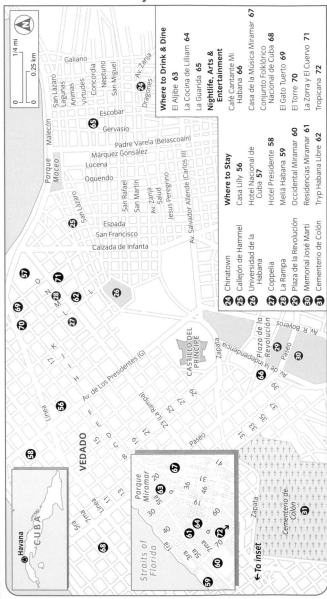

Where to Drink & Dine
El Aljibe **63**
La Cocina de Lilliam **64**
La Guarida **65**

Nightlife, Arts & Entertainment
Café Cantante Mi Habana **66**
Casa de la Música Miramar **67**
Conjunto Folklórico Nacional de Cuba **68**
El Gato Tuerto **69**
El Torre **70**
La Zorra y El Cuervo **71**
Tropicana **72**

Where to Stay
Casa Lilly **56**
Hotel Nacional de Cuba **57**
Hotel Presidente **58**
Meliá Habana **59**
Occidental Miramar **60**
Residencias Miramar **61**
Tryp Habana Libre **62**

24 Chinatown
25 Callejón de Hammel
26 Universidad de la Habana
27 Coppelia
28 La Rampa
29 Plaza de la Revolución
30 Memorial José Martí
31 Cementerio de Colón

Originally established in 1514 on Cuba's southern coast, San Cristóbal de la Habana had been moved by 1519 to its present location on the island's north, at the mouth of a deep and spacious harbor with a narrow, protected channel. Before long, Havana had become the most important port in the Spanish colonial empire. Today, it's a city of beauty and devastation. The colonial core has been restored, but much of its central residential areas reveal years of decay.

① Plaza de Armas. Surrounding the shaded urban park that now takes up the plaza, you can discover the Palacio de los Capitanes Generales (Palace of the Captain Generals) and Museo de la Ciudad (see ④), the Castillo de la Real Fuerza (see ③), El Templete (see ②), and the Hotel Santa Isabel, housed in the former palace of the Count of Santovenia. Most days, the square is lined with stands set up by used-book sellers.

② El Templete. A tall ceiba tree stands in front of this neoclassical Doric temple. The tree is the younger cousin of a fallen giant that stood here on the site where local citizens celebrated the town's first Mass in the early 1500s. Behind the tree stands the 'little temple,' built between 1754 and 1828. ⏱ *15 min.* C/ Baratillo and O'Reilly, Plaza de

La Giraldilla, Castillo de la Real Fuerza.

Second-hand book stall, Plaza de Armas.

Armas. ☎ 7/861-2876. Admission CUC$3. Daily 9am–6pm.

③ ★ kids Castillo de la Real Fuerza. This well-preserved, 16th-century fort sits within a broad cloverleaf moat. It is the oldest in Havana, and the oldest surviving fort in the Western hemisphere. Its most distinctive feature is the weather-vane, **La Giraldilla,** which has come to be the city's defining symbol. Today, the fort contains brand-new exhibits of items salvaged from shipwrecks. ⏱ *30 min.* C/ O'Reilly 2 esq Av. del Puerto. ☎ 7/861-5010. Admission CUC$1. Tues–Sat 9.30am–5pm, Sun 9.30am–12.30pm.

④ ★★ Museo de la Ciudad. Housed inside this beautiful example of 18th-century Cuban baroque architecture is the city museum. The seat of Cuba's government for more

Ceramic ladies, Mercado Tacón.

than 100 years, the building now features a dozen or so rooms with polished marble floors and ornate architectural details, which have displays of colonial-era relics and artifacts. ⏱ *1 hr. C/ Tacón e/ C/ O'Reilly and Obispo.* ☎ *7/861-6130. Admission CUC$3. Daily 9am–6pm.*

5 Café O'Reilly. Although the bar and restaurant occupies two floors of this decaying building, all the action takes place on the second floor. French doors open onto a small veranda, affording a view of the folks strutting by on the street below. *C/ O'Reilly 203 esq C/ San Ignacio. $.*

6 ★★★ Catedral de San Cristóbal. The plaza fronting the cathedral and the church's baroque facade, with its asymmetrical towers, are the most visited attractions in La Habana Vieja. Inside, the cathedral is simple, almost to the point of austerity, thanks to a radical 19th-century neoclassical makeover. ⏱ *10 min. Plaza de la Catedral.* ☎ *7/861-7771.*

Free admission. Mon–Fri 11am–3pm, Sat 11am–2pm, Sun (Mass) 9.30am–12.30pm.

7 kids Mercado Tacón. The biggest and best street market in Havana. In addition to the typical arts and crafts and souvenir T-shirts, you can find scores of local painters selling their wares. *C/ Tacón e/ C/ Empedrado and Chacón. Wed–Sun 9am–6pm.*

8 ★ Centro Wifredo Lam. This little gallery is dedicated to the memory of Cuba's most treasured modern artist. The museum houses a sizable collection of Lam's lithographs and acrylic works, as well as works of art and sculpture from the artist's personal collection. ⏱ *25 min. C/ San Ignacio esq C/ Empedrado.* ☎ *7/861-3419. Admission CUC$2. Mon–Sat 10am–5pm.*

9 Cafetería El Portal. With seating on the large covered patio, and a couple of dozen tables set right on the Plaza de la Catedral, few places have more character in La Habana

Vieja than this café. Perfect for a drink and light meal, day or night. *Plaza de la Catedral.* ☎ 7/867-1034. $–$$.

⑩ Plaza Vieja. The oldest plaza in Havana was first laid out in 1599 and was dubbed 'Plaza Nueva' (New Square). It soon lost prominence to the better located Plaza de Armas and Plaza de la Catedral. At the center of the broad open square is a replica of an 18th-century fountain.

⑪ Plaza de San Francisco. This is the most open and uncluttered plaza in La Habana Vieja, anchored by the **Fuente de los Leones** (Lion's Fountain), sculpted in 1836 by Italian Giuseppe Gaggini. The imposing facade of the **Lonja de Comercio** (Stock Exchange) dominates the northern side. The southern edge is defined by the 16th-century **Basílica Menor de San Francisco de Asís.** Be sure to climb the bell tower here, the tallest church tower in Havana, for the

Plaza de San Francisco.

El Portal, Plaza de Catedral.

view. 🕐 *20 min. Plaza de San Francisco.* ☎ *7/862-9683. Admission CUC$2. Daily 9am–6pm.*

⑫ Calle Obispo. The busiest and most distinctive street in La Habana Vieja. This bustling pedestrian-only boulevard connects Parque Central with the Plaza de Armas, making it the classic route for any walking tour of La Habana Vieja.

⑬ ★★ Museo Nacional de Bellas Artes. The National Fine Arts Museum houses a collection of Cuban art and sculpture. Modern masters such as Wifredo Lam, Raúl Martínez, Amelia Peláez, and Rene Portocarrero are well represented. 🕐 *2 hrs. C/ Trocadero e/ C/ Zulueta and Monserrate.* ☎ *7/861-0241. www.museonacional.cult.cu. Admission CUC$5. Tues–Sat 10am–6pm, Sun 10am–2pm.*

⑭ Museo de Arte Universal. This international collection is now housed in a restored, early-20th-century gem of a building. This selection leans heavily on classical and neoclassical European works,

Museo de Arte Universal.

with some fine portraits and still-lifes from the Dutch Golden Age. 🕐 1–2 hrs. C/ San Rafael e/ C/ Zulueta and Monserrate. ☎ 7/861-0241. www.museonacionalcult.cu. Admission CUC$5. Tues–Sat 10am–6pm, Sun 10am–2pm.

15 **Café La Barrita.** Tucked into a second-floor nook of a spectacular art-deco building, the café provides red leather chairs from which to admire the bat-decorated light shades and door handles. Sandwiches, salads, and drinks are available. *Edificio Bacardí, Monserrate 261 esq C/ San Juan de Dios.* ☎ 7/862-9310 ext 131. $.

16 ★ **Museo de la Revolución y Memorial Granma.** Housed in the former Presidential Palace, the Museum of the Revolution and the Granma Memorial outline Cuba's history in minute detail, with an emphasis on its independence and revolutionary struggles. There's a stunning replica of Versailles' Hall of Mirrors, ornate bas-relief work, and interior decorations by Tiffany. Outside, tanks and planes surround the glass-enclosed *Granma*, the 23.6-m) (59-foot) motor launch that carried Fidel Castro, Che Guevara, and 80 other fighters to the island in 1956. 🕐 1½–2 hrs. C/ Refugio 1 e/ C/ Monserrate and Zulueta. ☎ 7/862-4091. Admission CUC$5. Daily 10am–5pm.

17 ★★★ kids **El Malecón.** This oceanside pedestrian walkway stretches all the way from the Castillo de San Salvador de la Punta in

Cannon Curfew

The cañonazo (cannon blast) is a picturesque ritual that takes place at **La Fortaleza de San Carlos de la Cabaña** every night (see **23**). An honor guard in 18th-century military garb emerges from the barracks at about 8.40pm and conducts a small parade to a bank of cannons overlooking Havana's harbor channel. With pomp and circumstance, the cannon is loaded and fired at precisely 9pm. About 1,000 people show up each night, the vast majority of them Cubans. Arrive early if you want a good vantage point. The blast itself is quite loud—you can hear it across Havana—so protect your ears. You can combine the ceremony with a meal at one of the nearby restaurants.

La Habana Vieja to the Almendares River that separates Vedado from Miramar (about 7km (4½ miles) in total). Everybody strolls and lingers along the Malecón, which is the social center, day and night, for a cross-section of Cubans.

18 Parque Central. This park, dominated by a marble statue of José Martí, marks the western boundary of La Habana Vieja. Parque Central is a popular local gathering spot, particularly known for its heated conversations about baseball. Classic hotels ring the park, including the Hotel Inglaterra and Hotel Plaza (p 99).

19 ★ kids Prado. Paseo de Martí, or Prado, features El Capitolio (see 20) and the Gran Teatro de la Habana on its western edge and the Palacio del Centro Asturiano, which holds the international collection of the Museo Nacional de Bellas Artes (see 13), on its eastern. North of the *parque central*, Prado contains a pedestrianized tiled promenade adorned by lamps that leads back to the Malecón (see 17).

20 ★ El Capitolio. Modeled after its US cousin, the Cuban Capitol is a stunning architectural work of grandiose scale. The entrance hall has a replica of a 25-carat diamond imbedded in the floor, from which all highway distances radiating out from Havana are measured. There's also the Statue of the Republic, a 17m-tall (56-foot), 48-tonne Roman goddess covered in gold leaf. ⏲ *1½ hrs. Prado e/ C/ San José and Dragones.* ☎ *7/861-5519. Admission CUC$3. Daily 9am–6pm.*

21 ★ Fábrica de Tabaco Partagás. Founded in 1845, this is Cuba's largest and most renowned cigar factory, producing around 5 million cigars every year. The neoclassical facade is especially resplendent in the Havana morning sunlight.

Official tours are held at 10am and 2pm daily, although you can sometimes work your way into one of the many tour groups that pass through all day. Their well-stocked shop, **La Casa del Habano,** is open all day. ⏲ *1 hr. C/ Industria 524 (behind El Capitolio).* ☎ *7/862-4604. 45-min. guided tour CUC$10. Tickets must now be purcahsed at Cubatur offices inside nearby hotels. Mon–Sat 9.30–11am, 12.30–2.30pm.*

22 ★★ Parque Histórico Morro y Cabaña (Castillo del Morro). This historic park of forts, battlements, and barracks was responsible for the protection of Havana for centuries. 'El Morro' was built between 1589 and 1630. In addition to its ramparts, barracks, and banks of cannons, El Morro has a series of exhibition rooms. You can walk the fort's ancient streets and even climb the still-functioning, 19th-century

A classic car parked outside Gran Teatro, Prado.

lighthouse. 🕐 *1½–2 hrs. Carretera de La Cabaña, Habana del Este.* ☎ *7/863-7063. Admission CUC\$3. Daily 8am–8pm.*

㉓ ★★ Parque Histórico Morro y Cabaña (La Fortaleza de San Carlos de la Cabaña). La Fortaleza de San Carlos de la Cabaña was built between 1764 and 1774, as a response to the British invasion. The long fort is a miniature city with a high perch overlooking the harbor channel and La Habana Vieja. It features the **Comandancia de Che Guevara,** a room where the revolutionary leader briefly set up a command post after storming the fort in January 1959. Stop in at the cigar shop, which features the longest cigar in the world, an 11-m (36-foot) stogie that hangs above your head and is duly registered in the Guinness Book of World Records. 🕐 *1½–2 hrs. Carretera de La Cabaña, Habana del Este.* ☎ *7/862-0617. Admission CUC\$3 before 6pm, CUC\$5 after 6pm. Daily 10am–midnight.*

㉔ Chinatown. Occupying a small section of Centro Habana, the city's Chinatown has few distinguishing features and a very small population of residents of Chinese descent, but

Murals cover the wall in Callejón de Hammel.

it is a curious anomaly with its Chinese street signs and other accents. A block-long pedestrian-only street, El Cuchillo de Zanja, is packed with nondescript and unimpressive Chinese restaurants and shops. The biggest attraction here is the large, pagoda-style Dragon's Gate at the corner of Calle Dragones and Calle Amistad. Chinatown is in the area bordered by Calles Dragones, Zanja, Rayo and San Nicolás.

㉕ ★★★ kids Callejón de Hammel. Nearly every inch of this narrow, 2-block-long alleyway is painted in bright colors, the work of painter Salvador González. Most are mural-size depictions of Afro-Cuban deities. There are also sculptures made from scrap and old bike parts, as well as a Nganga, a sacred place for the celebration of Palo Monte rituals centered on a giant cauldron. At noon each Sunday, this is the site of a weekly Afro-Cuban music and dance show and celebration headed up by the renowned folkloric group Clavé y Guaguanco. 🕐 *1 hr.* See p 43.

㉖ Universidad de la Habana. The compact campus of Havana's main university sits on high ground in Vedado close to the former Havana Hilton (now Hotel Habana Libre). The broad staircase leading up to the school, with its signature Alma Mater statue of a seated woman with outstretched arms, is a popular gathering spot for students. You can sometimes catch impromptu concerts here. *C/ L and 27, La Ronda.* ☎ *7/879-3488.*

㉗ ★ kids Coppelia. Made famous by Tomás Gutiérrez Alea's hit film *Fresa y Chocolate* (*Strawberry and Chocolate*), this is the main branch of the Cuban national ice-cream company. At the center of the block-long complex is a postmodern

Coppelia.

building of curving concrete and glass, surrounded by a series of open courtyards with wrought-iron tables, where customers are served bowls of the frozen nectar. *C/ 23 and L.* ☎ *7/832-6184. Tues–Sun 11am–10pm.*

㉘ La Rampa. This main road and popular promenade leads to El Malecón (see ㉗) and is lined with cinemas, airline offices, and ministry buildings. At its main intersection is the Hotel Habana Libre (p 103) that headquartered Fidel after his 1959 victory. Closer to the sea and just off La Rampa is the historic Hotel Nacional with its imposing façade. *See p 103.*

㉙ Plaza de la Revolución. This enormous, brutalist square dominated by the José Martí memorial (see ㉚) is host to Cuba's political rallies. It's surrounded by the national theater and ministry buildings including the Ministry of Interior building with the iconic image of Che Guevara's face cast in iron. *Plaza de la Revolución, Nuevo Vedado.*

㉚ Memorial José Martí. The 109-m (358-foot) marble tower here is the highest point in Havana. At

the base of the tower is a massive statue of the poet and national independence hero José Martí. Inside the base is a small museum dedicated to Martí. The lookout is by far the most interesting and popular attraction here. 🕐 *45 min. Plaza de la Revolución, Nuevo Vedado.* ☎ *7/859-2347. Admission museum CUC$3; mirador CUC$2. Mon–Sat 9am–5pm.*

㉛ ★★ Cementerio de Colón. A miniature city of mausoleums, crypts, family chapels and vaults, soaring sculptures, and ornate gravestones, Columbus Cemetery covers 55 hectares (136 acres). Designed by Spanish architect Calixto de Loira in the mid-1800s, it's laid out in grids around a central chapel. The main entrance features a large sculpture of Faith, Hope, and Charity in Carrara marble. There's also a large monument to fallen soldiers of the Revolutionary Armed Forces, and an impressive stainless steel sculpture capping a memorial to the martyrs of the 1957 attack on Batista's Presidential Palace. 🕐 *1–2 hrs. C/ Zapata and 12.* ☎ *7/832-1050. Admission CUC$1. Daily 8am–5pm. Guided tours available.*

Where to Stay: **La Habana Vieja**

Casa Eduardo Canciano A second-floor apartment in a central location run by a friendly family. It has a wonderful Sevillana patio and Spanish wooden colonial windows. The large bedroom equipped with air-conditioning and a fan has an adjoining, original jet-black-and-yellow bathroom. The dining room is next to the sweet balcony overlooking the street. *C/ Refugio 103 e/ C/ Prado and Morro. ☎ 7/863-0523. www.winpict.com/cuba/index.htm. eduardo.canciano@infomed.sld.cu. Two rooms. CUC$25–30 double. No credit cards.*

Casa Mary A tastefully decorated second-floor apartment with an enormous terrace overlooking El Morro, next to the Spanish Embassy in a quiet location. The two small rooms have doors opening out onto the terrace, where you may lounge on painted iron chairs. *C/ Cárcel-Capdevila 59, 2nd floor, e / C/ Morro and Zulueta. ☎ 7/861-5911. http://xoomer.alice.it/gianni_franci. mariange2850@yahoo.com. Two rooms. CUC$35 double. No credit cards.*

Chez Nous A friendly couple rent out this homely apartment, which is a stone's throw from Plaza Vieja. The two rooms share a bathroom and there's a great terrace for sun lounging. *C/ Teniente Rey 115 e/ C/ Cuba and San Ignacio. ☎ 7/862-6287. cheznous@ceniai.inf.cu. Two rooms. CUC$30 double. No credit cards.*

★ Hotel Ambos Mundos This popular hotel with a Hemingway connection (p 35) is a good base for exploring La Habana Vieja. Rooms are simple and somewhat spartan, but they are comfortable, and most have high French doors opening to some views of the bustling streets. *C/ Obispo 153 esq C/ Mercaderes. ☎ 7/860-9530. www.habaguanexhotels.com. 52 rooms. CUC$110–163 double w/breakfast. MC, V.*

★ Hotel Conde de Villanueva This place is so geared towards cigar freaks that only true aficionados should stay here. The rooms are large and soaked in old-world charm, not to mention the scent of tobacco—all are smoking rooms, of

Barrios: La Habana Vieja

La Habana Vieja (Old Havana) is the historic Spanish colonial heart of Havana. Situated at the eastern edge of the city, in the area beginning around the Paseo del Prado and the Parque Central, and extending to the Harbor Channel, it's a dense collection of colonial-era and neocolonial houses, mansions, churches, seminaries, and apartment buildings punctuated by a few picturesque plazas and parks. UNESCO declared La Habana Vieja a World Heritage Site in 1982, and today it's one of the most beautiful restored colonial cities in the world, and an area best explored on foot.

Hotel Los Frailes.

wrought-iron beds, checkerboard marble floors, and tasteful framed prints. The tranquil central courtyard provides immediate relief, surrounded by soaring stone columns connected by high arches. *C/ Obispo esq C/ Cuba.* ☎ *7/862-4127. www.habaguanexhotels.com. 25 rooms. CUC$110–163 double w/breakfast. MC, V.*

★ **Hotel Los Frailes**   This is still a lovely little hotel located in the heart of La Habana Vieja. The rooms have high ceilings, smooth stucco walls, and heavy wooden beds. The narrow courtyard is engulfed in lush tropical foliage cascading down from the second-floor hallways, and features a murmuring fountain. *C/ Teniente Rey 8 e/ C/ Mercaderes and Oficios.* ☎ *7/862-9383. www.habaguanexhotels.com. 22 rooms. CUC$94–132 double w/breakfast. MC, V.*

★ **Hotel Plaza**   Built in 1909, this is one of the more historic hotels of La Habana Vieja. However, historic charm is in greater supply than

Hotel Raquel.

course. The building dates back to the end of the 18th century, and features a large portrait of its namesake count in the entryway. *C/ Mercaderes 202 e/ C/ Lamparilla and Amargura.* ☎ *7/862-9293. www.habaguanexhotels.com. Nine rooms. CUC$125–163 double w/breakfast. MC, V.*

★ **Hotel del Tejadillo**   Just a half-block from the Plaza de la Catedral and La Bodeguita del Medio, this renovated old mansion provides decent value and ample colonial charm. The spacious rooms have high ceilings and comfortable new beds. Most are set around a typical central courtyard, with a fountain surrounded by lush tropical plants. *C/ Tejadillo 12 esq C/ San Ignacio.* ☎ *7/863-7283. www.habaguanexhotels.com. 32 rooms. CUC$94–132 double w/breakfast. MC, V.*

★★ **Hotel Florida**   Built in 1836 and turned into a hotel in 1885, the Florida is stately and elegant. The rooms are decorated with a mix of imitation and real antique furnishings,

actual comfort or luxury; although rooms have attractive dark-wood furniture and the bathrooms have tubs, they are a little spartan. Come by for an afternoon drink at the rooftop Solarium Bar, with great views of Havana and the neighboring Bacardí building. *C/ Ignacio Agramonte 267.* ☎ *7/860-8583. www.gran-caribe. com. 188 rooms. CUC$120–160 double w/breakfast. MC, V.*

★ **Hotel Raquel** Known as the 'Jewish hotel,' this is another stunningly restored old building. The facade is a visual orgy of bas-relief work, while the centerpiece of the marble-tiled lobby is a soaring stained-glass atrium ceiling. The third-floor rooms share a large rooftop terrace, with rooftop views over Old Havana. *C/ Amargura, esq San Ignacio.* ☎ *7/860-8280. www.haba guanexhotels.com. 25 rooms. CUC$110–163 double w/breakfast. MC, V.*

★★ **Hotel Santa Isabel** An elegant and charming hotel bordering Plaza de Armas, but the rooms and bathrooms are rather compact. The best rooms in the house, aside from the sumptuous Santovenia suite,

Swimming pool terrace, Hotel Saratoga.

are nos. 304 through 314, which come with large rooftop terraces overlooking the plaza. *C/ Baratillo 9, Plaza de Armas.* ☎ *7/860-8201. www.habaguanexhotels.com. 27 rooms. CUC$152–266 double w/ breakfast. MC, V.*

★★★ **Hotel Saratoga** This hotel has the most luxurious rooms of any La Habana Vieja property. Even the standard rooms are very spacious, with marble or tile floors, elegant furnishings, and all the modern amenities. The best features here are the delightful rooftop pool with citywide views and probably the best hotel breakfast in Cuba. *Prado 603.* ☎ *7/868-1000. www.hotel-saratoga.com. 96 rooms. CUC$275–775 double. MC, V.*

★★ **Hotel Sevilla** An historic hotel decked in Andalucian tiles with an inviting street-level pool. Some of the standard rooms are a bit small and lackluster, and so it's definitely worth the splurge for a superior or junior suite—you get a lot more space. *C/ Trocadero 55 esq Prado.* ☎ *7/860-8560. www.mercure.com. 178 rooms. CUC$62–213 double w/ breakfast. MC, V.*

★ **La Casona de Obrapía** This restored, spacious colonial home is run by Reymond and Raydel. The rooms are interior—the first is en suite, and the second shares a bathroom. There's a rooftop terrace for lounging, a barbecue, and a Jacuzzi under the sun. There's attractive maroon, gray, and blue tiling throughout, a large living room with a balcony overlooking the street, and an interior patio with tables and chairs. *C/ Obrapía 405 e/ C/ Aguacate and Compostela.* ☎ *7/862-8285. reymond_15@yahoo.es. Two rooms. CUC$30–35 double. No credit cards.*

★★ **NH Parque Central** This modern, upscale hotel dominates the northern end of Havana's small

Central Park. Rooms are new and spacious; the marble bathrooms even have a separate bathtub and shower. The rooftop pool and views are a winner. *C/ Neptuno e/ C/ Prado and Zulueta.* ☎ *7/860-6627. www. nh-hotels.com. 227 rooms. CUC$270 double. MC, V.*

Park View Hotel An old hotel, originally opened in 1928, which has been entirely restored and remodeled. Rooms, though by no means large, are comfortable and inviting. Their biggest drawback is the small-ish bathrooms, which have slightly cramped corner shower units. *C/ Colón esq C/ Morro.* ☎ *7/861-3293. www.habaguanexhotels.com. 55 rooms. CUC$84–104 double w/breakfast. MC, V.*

Where to Stay: **Centro**

Casa Melba and Alberto.

★ **Casa Evora Rodríguez** Stunning views are enjoyed from the top-floor 'penthouse' of this apartment with wraparound windows. The Capitolio, El Morro, and the sea can all be viewed from the balconies. The first room is large with two double beds, a pink-tiled bathroom, and amazing double views of the city. The second has one double bed and a table and chairs as well as the fantastic views. Evora speaks good English. *Prado 20, 9th floor, e/ San Lázaro and Cárcel.* ☎ *7/861-7932. evorahabana@yahoo. com. Two rooms. CUC$35 double. No credit cards.*

Casa Federico y Yamelis Llanes A young couple, who trained as lawyers, run this modern apartment close to the Malecón. The two comfortable rooms (one

Barrios: **Centro**

In many ways, the Centro district is little more than the necessary and neglected area connecting La Habana Vieja with Vedado. It's defined on its northern edge by El Malecón. The stretch of El Malecón (and everything inland from it) between the Hotel Nacional and La Habana Vieja is a study in decay and decomposition. Still, it is picturesque and charming in its own way. Centro Habana is primarily a residential area, although it does have a high concentration of *casas particulares* (private rooms for rent).

Hotel Inglaterra.

much larger than the other) share an inter-connecting bathroom. The living room overlooks the Prado. Federico is a source of all kinds of advice. *C/ Cárcel 156 e/ C/ San Lázaro y Prado.* ☎ *7/861-7817. fllanes@gmail.com. Two rooms. CUC$25 double. No credit cards.*

★ **Casa Melba and Alberto** Welcoming Melba and Alberto offer two en suite rooms, one of which enjoys sweeping balcony views of the city. Downstairs there's an independent kitchen and living room in this well-run apartment. Don't let the state of the entrance and elevators put you off. *C/ Galiano 115,*

Apto 81, 8th floor, e/ C/ Animas and Trocadero. ☎ *7/863-5178. barracuda1752@yahoo.es. Two rooms. CUC$30 double. No credit cards.*

Hotel Inglaterra In business since 1875, this hotel is showing its age. The ornate lobby, with its colorful Moorish mosaics, and the lively streetside café are the best features here. Rooms are perennially desultory and dated, and most have small bathrooms. However, quite a few of the rooms do come with a small balcony overlooking the Parque Central. *Prado 416 (in front of Parque Central).* ☎ *7/860-8595. www.gran-caribe.com. 83 rooms. CUC$120 double w/breakfast. MC, V.*

★ **Hotel Telégrafo** This restored hotel is more than a century old, and yet it has the boldest and most contemporary architecture and interior design in town. The rooms have soaring high ceilings and a majority have views over Parque Central, although a few let out onto the interior courtyard. Unfortunately, the hyperhip interior design can end up leaving the rooms feeling a bit spartan and uninviting. *Prado 408 esq Neptuno.* ☎ *7/861-1010. www.habaguanex hotels.com. 63 rooms. CUC$110–163 double w/breakfast. MC, V.*

Where to Stay: **Vedado**

★ **Casa Lilly** On the 13th floor of a 1950s block, this enormous apartment affords spectacular views of the city. The rooms are large and attractively decorated and guests share a spacious, minimally decorated living room enhanced by Asian influences. Breakfasts are served up on the elegant long dining table or on the wraparound terrace. Run by Lilly and her family, who work in film, this is a gorgeous place to stay. *C/ G*

301 esq C/ 13, 13th floor. ☎ *7/832-4021. www.casalilly.com. Two rooms. CUC$30–40 double. No credit cards.*

★★ **Hotel Nacional de Cuba** Sitting on a high bluff overlooking El Malecón, this is Havana's signature hotel, and it's loaded with atmosphere. The rooms themselves are large although somewhat drab and showing their age. Over half have ocean views. The hotel has a vast lawn area that opens out toward

Hotel Nacional de Cuba.

the sea. This is a great place for a sunset drink, with giant cannons protecting you on either side. *C/ O esq C/ 21.* ☎ *7/873-3564. www.grancaribe.com. 457 rooms. CUC $142–CUC$172 double w/breakfast. MC, V.*

★★ **Hotel Presidente** An elegant Vedado hotel, whose impeccable Victorian-style lobby features black-and-white marble floors, pink marble wainscoting, and real antiques. Some of the standard rooms are a bit compact, while others are quite spacious. About half (generally the even-numbered rooms) have good ocean views. There's an outdoor pool on the

ground level, with a poolside bar and grill. *C/ Calzada 110 esq Av. de los Presidentes.* ☎ *7/838-1001. www.hotelesc.com. 158 rooms. CUC$140 double w/breakfast. MC, V.*

★★ **Tryp Habana Libre** Rising high above Havana from a spot on La Rampa, this hotel provides some superb views of the city and sea from most of its rooms. The rooms themselves are large and comfortable, although they feel dated, despite the fact that most of the carpets and furniture are new. *C/ L and 23.* ☎ *7/838-4011. www.solmelia cuba.com. 572 rooms. CUC$140–190 double w/breakfast. MC, V.*

Barrios: Vedado

Beginning more or less at the Hotel Nacional and extending west to the Almendares River, and south to the Plaza de la Revolución, Vedado is a busy mix of middle- to upper-class houses and businesses. As the older sections of La Habana Vieja and Centro Habana began to overflow, residential and business growth centered on Vedado. Calle 23, or La Rampa, is the principal avenue defining Vedado. The Plaza de la Revolución sits on high ground on the southern edge of Vedado and houses several government agencies, in addition to the towering José Martí Memorial, the National Theater, and the National Library.

Barrios: Playa

Playa is an upscale residential district located just west of Vedado, past the Almendares River. The most important neighborhood here is Miramar, home to many prominent businesses and most of the resident foreign community in Cuba. Almost all the various embassies and diplomatic missions have set up shop in the various Batista-era mansions that make up this neighborhood. There are several large and luxurious, business-class hotels here, as well as many private rooms for rent in neocolonial mansions.

Where to Stay: Playa

★★ **Meliá Habana** This modern luxury hotel is set on a coral ledge on the edge of the Caribbean. Its rows of balconies are draped with flowing ferns. Most of the rooms have excellent ocean views from their good-size private balconies. Rooms are large and comfortable, with high ceilings and big bathrooms. The hotel is the unofficial hub of the business scene in Miramar. *Av. 3 e/ C/ 76 and 80.* ☎ *7/204-8500. www.solmeliacuba.com. 397 rooms. CUC$220 double w/breakfast. MC, V.*

★★ **Occidental Miramar** This modern and massive luxury hotel is an impressive and imposing presence in the heart of Miramar's business district. The rooms are all at least junior suites. Although it's a

couple of blocks from the sea, it does have a nice swimming pool. *Av. 5 e/ C/ 72 and 76.* ☎ *7/204-3584. www.occidentalhotels.com. 427 rooms. CUC$130 double w/breakfast. MC, V.*

★ **Residencias Miramar** An excellent *casa particular* (private rooms for rent) decorated with handsome furnishings and with a wonderful host. Rooms are clean and modern, and each comes with its own phone and a small fridge. Common areas include a comfortable living room and a shady patio area amid well-tended gardens. Host Eva can help arrange tours and activities. *Av. 7 4403 e/ C/ 44 and 46.* ☎ *7/202-1075. evahabanasol@ yahoo.com. Two rooms. CUC$30 double. No credit cards.*

Where to Drink & Dine: La Habana Vieja

★ **Café del Oriente** *INTERNATIONAL* This elegant little restaurant on Plaza San Francisco has a few outdoor tables. Inside you'll find

a cool, large room, with a patterned marble floor and dark wainscoting on the walls. The menu is one of the most extravagant in Havana: wild rabbit with oregano and fish filet in lime coulis feature. *C/ Oficios 112 esq C/ Armargura.* ☎ *7/860-6686. Mains CUC$9–21. MC, V. Daily noon–midnight.*

Cafetería El Portal *CRIOLLA*
With seating on the large covered patio, and a couple of dozen small tables set right on the Plaza de la Catedral, it's hard to think of a spot with more character in La Habana Vieja. The menu is small, but this place is big on atmosphere. The only real splurge is the lobster supreme in a light vinaigrette. *Plaza de la Catedral.* ☎ *7/867-1034. Mains CUC$4–17. MC, V. Daily noon–midnight.*

★★ **El Templete** *INTERNATIONAL/ SEAFOOD* This is truly fine dining portside, with tables on the roadside overlooking the harbor and sophisticated interior dining inside. The eclectic menu notes dishes such as beef carpaccio with foie gras and red wine reduction, baby eels, and a delicious tuna crusted with sesame seeds and Marmitako sauce. *Av del*

La Dominica.

Puerto esq Narciso López. ☎ *7/866-8807. Mains CUC$8–30. MC, V. Daily noon–midnight.*

★★ **La Dominica** *ITALIAN* Skip the formal and stuffy seating inside and grab one of the outdoor tables

Helping Hands in Havana

Havana is slowly growing accustomed to helping visitors, but the lack of decent tourist information remains frustrating. **Infotur,** C/ Obispo, esq C/ Bernaza (☎ 7/866-3333; www.infotur.cu) is an official state-run tourist information agency. It doesn't really know how to offer good information, but it's a start, and there's nothing else. Infotur has offices and kiosks in strategic spots around town and at the airport. It can also reluctantly provide brochures and can usually help with reservations. Most branches have a selection of maps and local tourist guides and books for sale. There are also a handful of large, state-run tour agencies with desks at most hotels that offer city tours of varying flavors. These include **Havanatur** (☎ 7/204-8409; www.havanatur.cu), **Cubanacán** (☎ 7/208-6044; www.cubanacan.cu), and **Cubatur** (☎ 7/835-4155; www.cubatur. cu). In Havana, the recommended **San Cristóbal** agency (☎ 7/861-9171; www.viajessancristobal.cu) also provides city tours that include sociocultural itineraries not offered by other agencies.

La Taberna de la Muralla.

cooked al dente and served in big portions. Mains include *saltimbocca alla Romana* (veal scallops wrapped in sage and prosciutto ham). *C/ O'Reilly and Mercaderes.* ☎ *7/860-2918. Mains CUC$6–26. MC, V. Daily noon–11pm.*

★ **La Taberna de la Muralla** *GRILL* Havana's only brewpub is blessed with a beautiful setting on a corner overlooking Plaza Vieja. The simple menu is made up almost entirely of grilled-to-order pork, chicken or fish, or kabobs of chicken, shrimp or lobster. Order a pint of the home-brewed amber or dark beer and admire the copper brewing tanks behind the bar. *Plaza Vieja.* ☎ *7/866-4453. Mains CUC$4–8. MC, V. Daily noon–midnight.*

★ **Los Nardos** *INTERNATIONAL/ SPANISH* Los Nardos is a coopera-tive that serves up some of the larg-est and tastiest platters in Havana. Dine by candlelight on large wooden tables accompanied by a live band. The servings of food are enormous: huge lobster platters or chicken with plenty of vegetables at reason-able prices. Expect to wait to get in. *Prado 565 e/ Teniente Rey and*

under a canvas umbrella beside the old brick streets. There's a wood-burning oven turning out excellent thin-crust pizzas. The pastas are

Los Nardos sign.

Transport Tales

Local buses are essentially off-limits to tourists, but a new red coach, **HabanaBusTour** (☎ 7/831-7333; www.transtur.cu), runs on three routes with a hop-on/hop-off service for CUC$5 a day. The routes cover La Habana Vieja to the Plaza de la Revolución, Plaza de la Revolución to Marina Hemingway through Miramar, and Parque Central to Playas del Este. They run from 9am to 9.20pm daily. All schedules are marked at the bright red bus stops. Opt for the open-air double decker for the best views. Other options for getting around include: horse-drawn carriages; **Coco Taxis** (☎ 7/873-1411) with their round open-air two seaters powered by a motorcycle; and antique cars that range from a Ford Model T to a 1957 Chevy. Both the horse-drawn carriages and Coco Taxis cost from CUC$5 to CUC$10 per hour, with a minimum of around CUC$3. **Gran Car** (☎ 7/881-0992) is the reputable and only agent for antique-car rentals, which, with a driver, run from CUC$25 per hour.

Dragones. ☎ 7/863-2985. Mains CUC$5–14. No credit cards. Daily 11.30am–11.30pm.

★★ Roof Garden Restaurant

FRENCH/INTERNATIONAL Located on the top floor of the Hotel Sevilla is one of the finer restaurants in Havana, with arguably the most impressive setting. The high ceiling displays intricate bas-relief work and moldings and the room is ringed by floor-to-almost-ceiling windows and decked out with marble floors and huge chandeliers. The menu is adventurous: for example, king prawns in aged rum and a delicious lamb ragout (cordero estofado). The set three-course meal is good value. C/ Trocadero 55 esq Prado. ☎ 7/860-8560. Mains CUC$9–32. MC, V. Daily 7–10.30pm.

★ Santo Angel INTERNATIONAL

With a handful of outdoor tables right on the Plaza Vieja, as well as others on the broad covered veranda facing the plaza, this is one of the most atmospheric restaurants in Old Havana. The cuisine is an eclectic mix of international dishes; the lamb in red wine and honey is recommended. C/ Teniente Rey 60 esq C/ San Ignacio. ☎ 7/861-1626. Mains CUC$8–28. MC, V. Daily 11.30am–11pm.

Where to Drink & Dine:
Centro & Vedado

★ **El Aljibe** *CRIOLLA*   The fixed-price *pollo asado El Aljibe* is the way to go at this open-air restaurant. Served all-you-can-eat family style with white rice, black beans, fried plantain, French fries, and salad, the slow-roasted chicken comes in a wonderful, slightly sweet-and-sour garlic *mojo* (gravy) that goes well over the rice. *Av. 7 e/ C/ 24 and 26.* ☎ *7/204-1583. Reservations recommended. Mains CUC$10–24. MC, V. Daily noon–midnight.*

★★ **La Cocina de Lilliam** *CRIOLLA*   The elegant, softly lit outdoor garden seating here would be enough on its own to recommend this *paladar* (a restaurant in a private home), but the food is excellent as well. Chef Lilliam Domínguez has a deft touch. The menu varies, but if available order the *ropa vieja*, made with shredded lamb instead of the traditional beef. *C/ 48 no. 1311 e/ C/ 13 and 15.* ☎ *7/209-6514. Reservations recommended. Mains CUC$10–15. No credit cards. Sun–Fri noon–3pm, 7–10pm.*

★★ **La Guarida** *CRIOLLA*   The most famous *paladar* in Cuba, known for its ambience, excellent cuisine, and starring role in the Cuban film *Fresa y Chocolate*. *Caimanero* (fresh red grouper) might come in a white-wine, orange, or sweet-and-sour sauce—all are good, as is the honey-lemon chicken and pork medallions in lemon sauce. *C/ Concordia 418 e/ C/ Gervasio and Escobar.* ☎ *7/866-9047. www. laguarida.com. Reservations required. Mains CUC$8–14. No credit cards. Daily noon–4.30pm, 7pm–midnight.*

La Cocina de Lilliam.

Homestay

A *casa particular* is a private house authorized to rent out two rooms housing two adults and children under 18 in each. The house should display a sticker—a bent blue capital 'H' set on its side stating Arrendador Divisa—declaring it to be a government-sanctioned casa. On arrival, casa owners must ask for your passport and enter the information into a registration book; you will be asked to sign next to it. Most houses are quite modest—you essentially live with a Cuban family. Rooms either have their own private hot-water bathroom or a bathroom shared with other tourists. Most rooms have air-conditioning. The minimum facilities you receive are clean sheets, towels, soap and toilet paper. Most houses provide locked rooms with a key. Most also serve huge meals at very reasonable prices and offer practical advice and a laundry service.

Havana Nightlife, Arts & Entertainment

Café Cantante Mi Habana
VEDADO   Top acts often perform at this popular club. They also have a much more informal dance scene every afternoon 4–7pm. This is a place where locals come to mix it up with foreigners who are in town to learn how to salsa. *Teatro Nacional, Paseo and C/ 39, Plaza de la Revolución.* ☎ *7/878-4275. Cover CUC$5–10.*

★★ Casa de la Música Centro Habana CENTRO   This place, with its massive dance floor and concert space in the heart of Centro Habana, is currently considered the best salsa-dancing venue in town. The crowd is predominantly Cuban, and most of the folks can really dance. About half of the cover is usually applied to your drink tab. *C/ Galiano 225, e/ Neptuno and Concordia.* ☎ *7/860-8296. Cover CUC$5–20.*

★★ Casa de la Música Miramar MIRAMAR   Housed in a beautiful, former Masonic Lodge Hall, this place has nightly concerts that range from bolero to salsa to jazz in the in-house club, Diablo Tun Tun. The real treat here is the afternoon jam sessions, which take place daily 4–7pm. *C/ 20 esq C/ 35, Miramar.* ☎ *7/204-0447. CUC$5–20.*

★★ Conjunto Folklórico Nacional de Cuba (Cuban National Folklore Group)
VEDADO   The weekly Sábado de la Rumba is a mesmerizing show of Afro-Cuban religious and secular dance and drumming held in an open-air courtyard. Two-hour show every Saturday at 3pm. *El Gran Palenque, C/ 4, e/ Calzada and Av 5, Vedado.* ☎ *7/830-3060. Cover CUC$5.*

★★ Cuban National Ballet
CENTRO   These dancers have been

Casa Reservations

If you have a reservation for your casa, your hosts should honor it. If you just turn up without a reservation and the house is full, the owner will farm you out to a friend or relative at a nearby house. You are under no obligation to take these places, but they can save you a lot of hassle. Make sure that they're legal houses, though. Even with a reservation, it's wise to make a follow-up confirmation by email or phone. Casa owners are happy to phone ahead to your next casa to tell the future host you're on your way. Be aware that if you show up at a *casa particular* (private rooms for rent) on the recommendation of a taxi driver or *jinetero*, either of them receives a commission of CUC$5, which invariably is indirectly added onto the bill. Note that casas can't accept bank cards, only cash.

garnering international accolades for decades, under the seemingly eternal direction of Alicia Onso. The major venue for the ballet is the Gran Teatro de La Habana, which is also a prime venue for concerts and dance performances. Other classical performing arts are staged at the Teatro Nacional de Cuba. *Gran Teatro, Prado and C/ San Rafael, Centro Habana.* ☎ *7/861-3077, ext. 115. www.balletcuba.cult.cu. Teatro Nacional, Paseo and C/ 39, Vedado.* ☎ *7/879-3558. Admission for foreigners CUC$20.*

★ **El Gato Tuerto** VEDADO This hyperhip little club attracts a good mix of travelers and Cuban intelligentsia. The mood is dark, with walls of mirrors behind the tiny stage, and a long bar running the length of the wall. Entertainment runs the gamut from old-style bolero to *nueva trova* and modern jazz. The admission is applied to your first drink, so ask for the *call liquor* (brand-name alcohol) first. *C/ O e/ 17 and 19, Vedado.* ☎ *7/838-2696. Cover CUC$5.*

El Torre VEDADO Not a particularly inviting space for barflies, but the views it enjoys of the Hotel Nacional and the gentle curve of the Malecón are cinematic, panoramic, and unrivaled. *Edificio Focsa, C/ 17 esq M, Vedado.* ☎ *7/832-7306.*

★★ **La Zorra y El Cuervo** VEDADO The premier jazz club in Havana and the first place to check if you want to catch any of the A-list jazz performers while you're in town. Modeled after an English pub, the basement-level bar space is small and cozy and relatively plain. The standard cover might double if someone like Chucho Valdés is playing. *La Rampa, C/ 23 155 e/ C/ N and O.* ☎ *7/833-2402. Cover CUC$10.*

★ **Lluvia de Oro** HABANA VIEJA A raucous and rowdy bar in the heart of Old Havana. There's often live music and a lively mix of tourists, locals, *jineteros*, and *jineteras*. *C/ Obispo 316 esq C/ Habana.* ☎ *7/ 862-9870.*

★★★ **Tropicana** MARIANAO First opened in 1939, this open-air dinner theater is still the defining

Tropicana, Havana.

Drinking

Most Cubans simply drink water or any number of popular soft drinks, including Sprite and Coca-Cola, whose locally produced equivalents are called Cachito and Tu Cola, respectively. One of the more interesting nonalcoholic drinks is guarapo, the sweet juice of freshly pressed sugar cane.

Cubans also drink plenty of coffee, and they like to brew it strong. Order café espresso for a straight shot, or café con leche if you'd like it mixed with warm milk. Ask for café americano if you want a milder brew.

Cuba produces a small handful of pretty good lager beers. Cristal, Bucanero, and Mayabe are the most popular. Cuba does produce excellent rums. The most well-known rums are Havana Club and Ron Santiago. In general, an aged rum (Añejo) is better than a white rum. Most visitors soon have their fill of mojitos (light rum with lime juice, fresh mint, sugar, and club soda) and daiquiris. Another popular cocktail is the cuba libre ('Free Cuba'), which is simply a rum and Coke with lime.

cabaret show in Cuba. Dinner starts at 8pm and is an uninspired but acceptable affair. The show follows at 10.30pm: the stage becomes an orgy of light, color, spectacular costumes, and pulsating movement. *C/ 72 e/ C/ 41 and 45. ☎ 7/267-0110. www.cabaret-tropicana.com. Show CUC$70–90. Packages available from tour operators with transport included. Packages are only slightly more than for the show alone, and so represent a decent deal.*

Tropical Nights

Unfortunately, comprehensive printed listings information in Cuba is nonexistent. For entertainment events, try the excursions desks of major hotels, because they carry flyers. For the national ballet, the *cartelera* (weekly events) is posted on the inside of the columns of the **Gran Teatro** on Parque Central. Before leaving home check www.cubaabsolutely.com, which lists events monthly, and www.cult.cu/paginas/index.php. The **Casa de la Música** in Centro posts its *cartelera* in the window, but also check http://promociones.egrem.co.cu/ for the weekly line up of all Egrem-run venues countrywide. Check the *cartelera* link on www.opushabana.cu for classical music and other events in Old Havana.

Baracoa

Havana
CUBA
Baracoa

| 0 | 100 yd |
| 0 | 100 m |

✉ Post Office

ATLANTIC OCEAN

Malecón

Antonio Maceo

José Martí

1 de Abril

Máximo Gómez

10 de Octubre

Maraví

Frank País

P. Cuervo

Parque Infantil

Malecón

Flor Crombet

Calixto García

R. Trejo

Ciro Frías

Rupert López

Céspedes

Coroneles Galano

Antonio Maceo

Félix Ruene

Plaza Martí

José Martí

Rodney Coutín

Roberto Reyes

Lumbano Sánchez

López Peña

Calixto García

Abel Díaz

Antonio Maceo

Moncada

1 El Castillo de Santa Bárbara

2 Fuerte de la Punta

3 Fuerte Matachín

4 La Punta

5 Nuestra Señora de la Asunción

6 Parque de la Independencia

7 Museo Arqueológico

8 El Yunque

9 Parque Nacional Alejandro de Humboldt

10 Playa Maguana

Where to Stay & Dine

Casa Daniel Salomón Paján 11

Casa Tropical 12

Hostal La Habanera 13

Hotel El Castillo 14

La Colonial 15

Villa Maguana 16

Swathed in tropical vegetation and refreshed by 10 rivers, Baracoa is the most picturesque spot in all Cuba. The historic town sits on an oyster-shaped bay, Bahía de Miel (Honey Bay), while a landmark flat-topped mountain looms in the background. Not only is Baracoa the most beautiful place on the island, it's also the oldest. Baracoa was the first settlement established by Diego Velázquez in 1511—making it the oldest colonial city in the Americas. The town shines during the first week of April, when street parties commemorate the date General Antonio Maceo disembarked at Playa Duaba in 1895, the beginning of Cuba's War of Independence.

Baracoa on the Bahía de Miel.

❶ ★ El Castillo de Santa Bárbara. In the 18th and 19th centuries, Baracoan settlers built three fortresses to protect the town from pirate attacks. **El Castillo de Santa Bárbara,** the oldest of the bunch, sits high above town, with splendid views of the bay and surrounding countryside; it has been converted into a hotel. *See p 115.*

❷ Fuerte de la Punta. Facing the seaside promenade, this exposed fort is now a restaurant; it sustained significant damage from the 2008 hurricanes, as did the town's Malecón.

❸ Fuerte Matachín. Close to the entrance to town, this distinctive fort, equipped with cannon, houses the municipal museum, Museo Matachín. Its exhibits relate to the town's history and its legends and myths. There's also a collection of extraordinary, vividly colored polimitas (snail shells). ⏲ *20 min. C/ Martí s/n esq Malecón.* ☎ *21/64-2122. Admission CUC$1. Daily 8am–noon, 2–6pm.*

❹ La Punta. On a covered terrace within the walls of one of the original three forts, this state-run restaurant is an elegant, tranquil spot, perfect for a break. The menu is varied. *Malecón final.* ☎ *21/64-5224. $.*

Cruz de la Parra, Nuestra Señora de la Asunción.

Catedral de Nuestra Señora de la Asunción and Hatuey statue.

⑤ Nuestra Señora de la Asunción. The rather austere and dilapidated cathedral was constructed in 1511, though it was burned by the French in 1652. The current structure was rebuilt at the beginning of the 19th century. It is most notable for the **Cruz de la Parra,** a small wooden cross on display inside a glass case. Locals insist that Columbus himself planted the cross on the banks of the bay in 1492, shortly after disembarking on Cuban soil for the first time. ⏱ *20 min. Maceo 152.* ☎ *21/64-3352. Free admission. Tues–Sat 8am–noon, 2–4pm.*

⑥ Parque de la Independencia. This park next to the church (also called Parque Central) is a popular gathering spot. A bust of the rebel Taíno Indian leader Hatuey (whose countenance today appears on beer bottles) adorns the square. Hatuey took up arms against the early *conquistadores* until he was caught by the Spanish and burned at the stake.

⑦ Museo Arqueológico. Around Baracoa there are as many as 50 pre-Columbian archaeological sites related to the major Native American groups that inhabited the area (Siboney, Taíno, and Guanturabey). The remains of Taínos can be seen in a cave, in the museum above town, as well as in a random collection of ceramics and artifacts supposedly belonging to this pre-Columbian tribe. The museum is only really worth the entrance fee to climb to the mirador, where you can admire the entire bay; on a clear day, the vista is stunning. ⏱ *1 hr. Reparto Paraíso. Admission CUC$3. Mon–Fri 8am–6pm, Sat 8am–noon.*

⑧ ★★ El Yunque. Described in Spanish chronicles as an anvil-shaped, high (575m (1,886 feet)), and square mountain, El Yunque dominates the Baracoa landscape. Frequently bathed in mist, the flat-topped limestone mountain can be climbed in 4-hour round-trip. The slopes are a UNESCO Biosphere Reserve, home to scores of bird species and unique plants.

⑨ ★★★ Parque Nacional Alejandro de Humboldt. A UNESCO Natural World Heritage Site of mountainous rainforest with karst scenery. See p 64.

Playa Maguana.

⑩ ★ **Playa Maguana.** A peaceful place with picture-perfect golden sands. There's a small restaurant and sunbeds to hire. *22km (14 miles) from town on road to Moa.*

Where to **Stay & Dine**

Casa Daniel Salomón Paján

This downtown house is one of the friendliest casas in Cuba. Daniel works at the museum and knows a lot about Baracoa's history. He has one comfortable room with a large bathroom close to the home's central covered patio. *C/ Céspedes 28, e/ Rubert López and Maceo.* ☎ *21/64-2122. fifi@toa.gtm.sld.cu. One room. CUC$20 double. No credit cards.*

Casa Tropical   A colonial house

with an enormous blue porch and courtyard that has very comfortable rooms and is run by a friendly and welcoming family. The very tasty swordfish in coconut sauce is almost reason enough to stay. *C/ Martí 175.* ☎ *21/64-3437. Two rooms. CUC$20 double. No credit cards.*

★ Hostal La Habanera   This

downtown colonial structure is atmospheric, affordable, and a perfectly-located option. The rooms are all spacious, with high ceilings, bright-patterned bed linens, rattan headboards, sparkling tile floors, and tubs in the bathrooms. *C/ Maceo 68, esq C/ Frank País.* ☎ *21/64-5273. www.gaviota-grupo.com. 10 rooms. CUC$49 double w/breakfast. MC, V.*

★★ Hotel El Castillo   Perched

on a hill with the best views of Baracoa and the bay, and a picture-perfect pool, this hotel—the lower part of which inhabits an old fort—is the top place in town. The simple rooms don't quite measure up to the privileged location and general ambience, though they're of pretty good size, have colonial-style furnishings, and are set around the pool.

Advance reservations are essential in high season. *C/ Calixto García, Loma el Paraíso.* ☎ *21/64-5165. www.gaviota-grupo.com. 34 rooms. CUC$54–58 double w/breakfast. MC, V.*

★ La Colonial   *BARACOAN/ CRIO-*

LLA   This well-run place (the only *paladar* in town) in a lovely colonial home has no fixed menu; fish and shrimp cooked in *leche de coco* (coconut milk) are usually served. *Martí 123.* ☎ *21/64-5391. Mains CUC$7–9. Daily 11am–11pm. No credit cards.*

★★ Villa Maguana   This little

place is set on a private, pretty cove next to Playa Maguana, a 2km (1¼ mile) white-sand beach. The four villas with 16 rooms are large and charmingly rustic, like private cabins, with dark-wood furniture; balconies with chairs overlook the transparent water. *Carretera de Moa a Baracoa, Km 20.* ☎ *21/64-1204. www.gaviota-grupo.com. 16 rooms. CUC$70–75 double w/breakfast. MC, V.*

Villa Maguana, Playa Maguana.

Bayamo

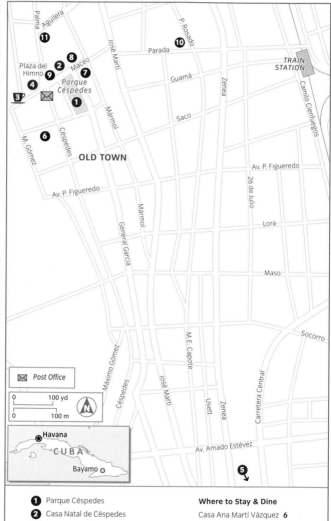

1 Parque Céspedes
2 Casa Natal de Céspedes
3 La Bodega
4 La Catedral del Santísimo Salvador
5 Gran Parque Nacional Sierra Maestra

Where to Stay & Dine

Casa Ana Martí Vázquez **6**
Casa Olga Celeiro Rizo **7**
Casa Rebeca Gómez Paneque **8**
Hotel Royalton **9**
Paladar El Polinesio **10**
Restaurant Sagitario **11**

Bayamo, one of Cuba's original seven villas (towns), is considered the birthplace of Cuban independence. The himno nacional (national anthem) was first sung here after the city was seized by the Liberating Army and became the capital of the Republic at Arms in 1869. South of Bayamo, the Sierra Maestra is where Fidel Castro and his band of rebels sneaked back into Cuba in 1956 after exile in Mexico. Today, Bayamo is a peaceful midsize city with little tourism and thus little hassle.

❶ ★ Parque Céspedes. This exquisite, peaceful square is flanked by tall royal palms. At one end of the plaza is a marble bust of the independence fighter Perucho Figueredo, which carries the words and music to 'La Bayamesa' (later the national anthem), imploring followers not to fear 'a glorious death' and encouraging Cubans that to 'die for the homeland is to live.' At the other end, is a stately granite and bronze statue of Carlos Manuel de Céspedes. Handsome, pastel-colored, arcaded colonial-style (post-1869) buildings ring the square.

❷ ★ Casa Natal de Céspedes. The birthplace of the 'father of the Cuban nation' is the only house on the square that escaped destruction in the 1869 fire. The significance of it alone being saved is not lost on Cubans. The two-story building hosts a chronological exhibit about the Céspedes family, elegant 19th-century colonial furnishings, and objects belonging to Céspedes (such as his ceremonial saber). The standout item, however, is the huge four-poster bronze bed complete with two oval shields depicting towns in mother-of-pearl decoration. Céspedes is remembered for refusing to trade his surrender for the life of his son, who was captured by the Spanish army; the Cuban patriot replied in writing that all Cubans were his sons and he could not be expected to trade their independence for the life of one

Wander the elegant furnishings in the Casa Natal de Céspedes.

man. The Spaniards promptly shot his son, Oscar. ⏱ *45 min. C/ Francisco Maceo Osorio 57.* ☎ *23/42-3864. Admission CUC$1. Tues–Fri 10am–6pm, Sat 10am–3pm, 8–10pm, Sun 10am–3pm, 8–10pm.*

❸ La Bodega. Huddled away behind the cathedral on Plaza del Himno, this little bar-cum-café-cum small restaurant enjoys sweeping views of the river. It's the loveliest place to kick back in town. *34 Plaza del Himno.* ☎ *23/42-1011. $.*

❹ La Catedral del Santísimo Salvador. This immense, ocher-colored 16th-century church that succumbed to the 1869 fire

La Catedral del Santísimo Salvador.

dominates Plaza del Himno. To one side of the cathedral, the small **Capilla de La Dolorosa** (Chapel of the Lady of Sorrows), which dates to 1740, is distinguished by a lovely Moorish-style, carved wooden ceiling and fine baroque altarpiece; it was only one of three important buildings to survive the 1869 blaze (the others were the Casa de la Trova and Céspedes' home). ⏱ *20 min. Plaza del Himno. No phone. Free admission. Daily 9am–1pm, 3–5pm.*

⑤ ★★ Gran Parque Nacional Sierra Maestra. Cuba's highest and longest mountain range stretches 140km (87 miles) west to east. Its highest peaks are only a few kilometers from the coastline, making for some exciting views for hikers. At its heart is **Parque Nacional de Turquino,** which includes Turquino, the nation's highest summit at just under 2,000m (6,562 feet).

Where to **Stay & Dine**

Casa Ana Martí Vázquez

A colonial home offering two rooms, each with a television, fridge, and air-conditioning. One room is reached by an extremely steep flight of stairs to a converted attic section, and so the other larger room is the preferred option. *C/ Céspedes 4 e/ Maceo and Canducha.* ☎ *23/42-5323. marti@enet.cu. Two rooms. CUC$20 double. No credit cards.*

Casa Olga Celeiro Rizo
This small, friendly household with two comfortable, air-conditioned rooms has a great terrace equipped with chairs overlooking the pleasant Francisco Maceo Osorio plaza. Host Olga can help with excursions. *C/ Parada 16 (Altos) e/ Martí and Mármol.* ☎ *23/42-3859. yaimara.grm@ infomed.sld.cu. Two rooms. CUC$20 double. No credit cards.*

Casa Rebeca Gómez Paneque

This centrally located 1930s house offers one large room with two beds, refrigerator, air conditioning, and fan in a quiet spot up some stairs at the back of the house. There's a sun terrace and interior patio plus a little library for relaxation. *Maceo 105 e/ Martí y Marmol.* ☎ *23/42-2327. One room. CUC$20–25 double. No credit cards.*

★ Hotel Royalton
Set facing Parque Céspedes, this charming hotel, dating to the 1940s, is currently undergoing refurbishment as a boutique hotel under the Islazul Hoteles E brand, and will be the top choice in town. Four of the rooms have small balconies with great plaza views. Off to one side of the lobby is the dependable Restaurant Plaza, which has a nice sidewalk

terrace and serves a generous plate of fried chicken with excellent fries, as well as chicken fricassee and beef with garlic sauce. *C/ Maceo 53.* ☎ *23/42-2290. www.islazul.cu. 33 rooms. CUC$29–35 double w/breakfast. Prices will rise once refurbishment is complete. MC, V.*

Paladar El Polinesio *CRIOLLA*
Grab a perch upstairs on the terrace overlooking the street of this private, sky-blue painted house. Dine on pork, Uruguayan steaks, or fish fillet accompanied by large portions of vegetables and rice. Service is very efficient. *Parada 125 e/ Pío Rosado and Capotico Bayamo.* ☎ *23/42-3860. Mains CUC$6–8. No credit cards. Daily noon–10pm.*

★ **Restaurant Sagitario** *CRIOLLA*
This place serves large and well-prepared meals in a pleasant backyard patio. The house specialty is pork steak cooked with cheese; the *pargo* (red snapper) is also good. Service here is friendly and downright efficient. *C/ Mármol 107 e/*

Casa Rebeca Gómez Paneque.

Maceo and Francisco Vicente Aguilera. ☎ *23/42-2449. Mains CUC$6–7. No credit cards. Daily noon–11pm.*

Grito de Yara

Bayamo grew wealthy in the 17th and 18th centuries from contraband, sugar, and cattle. Many of the local elite sent their young men to Spain and France to study, and some returned with enlightened ideals about colonialism and a desire for Cuban independence. Carlos Manuel de Céspedes (1819–74) was a wealthy businessman who, in 1868, freed his slaves and formed a small army that set about achieving that goal. The movement was known as the *Grito de Yara,* a call for independence or death. His forces captured Bayamo and gave life to the War of Independence against Spain. The rebels held Bayamo for three months until it became evident that the superior numbers of Spanish troops would defeat them. Rather than surrender, the rebel army burnt the city in 1869, the ultimate act of sedition. Most of Bayamo was wiped out by the self-immolation. A plaque marks the spot where the fire was started just off the southern corner of Parque Céspedes on Calle Guamá.

Camagüey

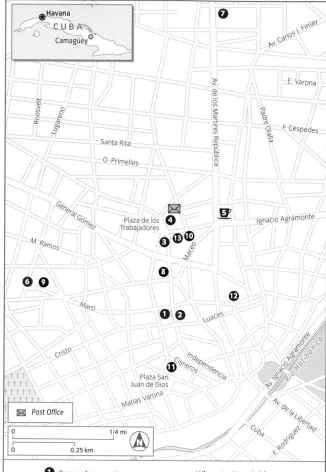

Where to Stay & Dine

1. Parque Agramonte
2. Artists' Studio
3. Casa Natal del Mayor (Ignacio Agramonte)
4. Iglesia de Nuestra Señora de La Merced
5. Callejón de la Soledad
6. Plaza del Carmen
7. Museo Provincial General Ignacio Agramonte

Casa Manolo Banegas **8**
El Ovejito **9**
Gran Hotel **10**
La Campana de Toledo **11**
Los Vitrales **12**
Restaurant Isabella **13**

Camagüey retains a strong colonial imprint, with a highly irregular layout and warren of narrow, bending streets and alleyways, handsome houses, and two of the most dignified plazas in Cuba. Founded as the sixth of Cuba's original seven villas in 1514—as a port town originally named Santa María del Puerto del Príncipe—the city was later moved to a different spot by Diego Velázquez in 1516 and transplanted again to its present, inland location in 1528.

❶ Parque Agramonte. At the center of this park is an equestrian statue of the city's most famous citizen, Ignacio Agramonte. Each corner of the park is marked by a tall royal palm, planted to pay tribute to local martyrs of the struggle for independence executed here by Spanish forces. The park is flanked by colonial houses, including the **Casa de la Trova** and the early-18th-century cathedral dedicated to **Nuestra Señora de la Candelaria.** *Cathedral:* 🕐 *30 min.* ☎ *32/29-4960. Admission CUC$1 to climb tower. Mon–Fri 8–11.45am, 2–5pm, Sat 3–4pm, Sun 8–11.30am.*

❷ Artists' Studio. The work of the amiable husband–wife team Joel Jover and Ileana Sánchez includes enormous iconic images of the Virgin Mary using the flattened cans of Cuban's national *cerveza* (beer) factory. The couple also have a gallery on Plaza San Juan de Dios. *C/ Martí 154, Parque Agramonte.* ☎ *32/29-2305. jover@pprincipe.cult.cu.*

❸ Casa Natal del Mayor (Ignacio Agramonte). Ignacio Agramonte y Loynaz, Camagüey's favorite son and the national hero of the independence struggle—known to all as 'El Mayor'—was born 23 December, 1841, in this distinguished 18th-century house. Agramonte's birthplace displays classical colonial elements, both baroque and Hispanic-mudéjar. There are carved wooden ceilings and period furnishings. 🕐 *30 min. C/ Ignacio*

Agramonte 459. ☎ *32/29-7116. Admission CUC$2. Tues–Sat 10am–5pm, Sun 8am–noon.*

❹ ★ Iglesia de Nuestra Señora de La Merced. The most significant structure on the plain Plaza de los Trabajadores is this 18th-century brick church, Camagüey's most distinguished and, in its day, the largest in Cuba. A chapel existed on this spot in 1601; the present structure dates from 1748 (it was reconstructed in 1848 and again in 1909 after a fire). Adorning the ceiling are surprising

Parque Agramonte.

Plaza del Carmen.

min. Av. Agramonte 4. ☎ *32/29-2783. Free admission. Tip to see the catacombs, because they're pad-locked. Mon–Sat 8am–1.30pm, 3–5pm, Sun 8am–1pm, 4.30–6pm.*

🟏 **Callejón de la Soledad.** This small shaded patio café with tables and umbrellas is a great ref-uge for watching the action on Av. República. *Next to Av. República 79. $.*

❻ ★★ **Plaza del Carmen.** A pedestrian-only street of pastel-col-ored colonial houses opens onto an irregularly shaped square. The revamped 18th-century square fea-tures street lamps, huge *tinajones* (clay pots that stored water), and larger-than-life sculptures of locals. The baroque-style **Iglesia de Nues-tra Señora del Carmen** dates from 1825 and is the only church in the eastern half of Cuba topped by two towers.

❼ **Museo Provincial General Ignacio Agramonte.** This museum, housing a collection of paintings, concentrates on Cuban fine arts (dating from the early 19th century). 🕓 *30 min. Av de los Már-tires 2 e/ Ignacio Sánchez and Rotario.* ☎ *32/28-2425. Admission CUC$2. Mon 1–5pm, Tues–Thurs, Sat 10am–5pm, Fri noon–7pm, Sun 10am–2pm.*

Art Nouveau murals. Also of note are the painted wood, neo-Gothic altar and the **Santo Sepulcro,** a 1762 casket elaborately fashioned from 25,000 silver coins and carried high by eight men during Easter pro-cessionals. Behind the principal altar is a crypt, the remains of an exten-sive underground cemetery. Six macabre tombs with skeletons remain and are on creepy view alongside a small museum of 18th- and 19th-century objects. 🕓 *30*

Where to **Stay & Dine**

★ **Casa Manolo Banegas** A gorgeous second-floor apartment stuffed with objets d'art, including an ancient Rigonda Bolshoi radio and possibly the largest hat-stand in the world. Both rooms have private bathrooms, although, as this is a colonial house, they're not en suite. A wraparound balcony and its great central location complete the appeal. *C/ Independencia 251, e/ Hermanos Agüero and Grl Gómez.* ☎ *32/29-4606. Two rooms. CUC$20 per room. No credit cards.*

★ **El Ovejito** *CRIOLLA* This restaurant specializes in lamb dishes, hence the name 'Little Lamb.' Heavy wooden tables and wood and rough-cowhide chairs are spread on the cobblestone plaza out-front and through several rooms of this lovingly restored home dating to 1827. Plaza del Carmen. *C/ Hermanos Agüero 152, e/ Onda and Carmen.* ☎ *32/24-2498. Mains CUC$2.10– 6.65. No credit cards. Daily noon–9.40pm.*

Gran Hotel Camagüey's classic hotel dates from 1939. Its clubby, old-world feel is accentuated by an abundance of watering holes—this midsize hotel has four bars. There's also a small pool. *C/ Maceo 67 e/ Grl Gómez and Ignacio Agramonte.* ☎ *32/29-2093. www.islazul.cu. 72 rooms. CUC$5–58 double w/breakfast. MC, V.*

★ **La Campana de Toledo** *CRIOLLA* This elegantly rustic restaurant ranks as the city's most enjoyable dining experience. The restored 18th-century house has a lovely patio and well-prepared dishes go beyond the standard offerings: try *picadillo a la Habanera* (beef hash), the house specialty. *San Juan de Dios 18 e/ Ramón Pinto and Padre Olallo.*

Gran Hotel.

Casa Manolo Banegas.

☎ *32/28-6812. Mains CUC$4.20–18. MC, V. Daily 11am–10pm.*

★ **Los Vitrales** A centrally located casa in a former seminary. The two en suite rooms are arrayed off the plant-filled patio courtyard and are spacious and quiet. Owner Rafael, an architect, is a mine of information about the area. *C/ Avellaneda 3 e/ General Gómez and Martí.* ☎ *32/29-5866. requejobarreto@gmail.com. Two rooms. CUC$20–25 double. No credit cards.*

★ **Restaurant Isabella** *ITALIAN* Named in honor of local actress Isabel Santos, this restaurant is a whirl of visual excitement and filmic ambience. If this isn't enough to entice you inside, the pizzas are huge and thin, don't scrimp on the ingredients, and are good value. *C/ Ignacio Agramonte e/ Independencia and Lopez Recio.* ☎ *32/22-1540. Mains CUC$2–8. No credit cards. Daily 11am–10pm.*

Cienfuegos

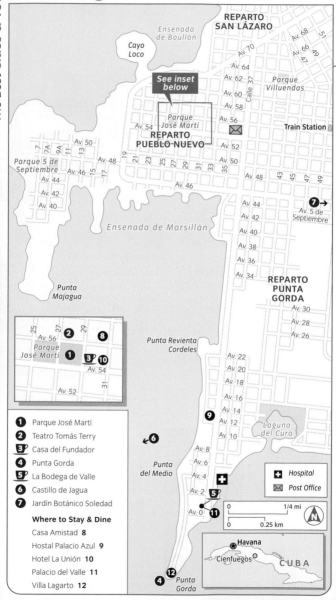

REPARTO SAN LÁZARO

Ensenada de Boullón

Cayo Loco

See inset below

Av. 70
Av. 68
51
Av. 66
49
Av. 47
Av. 64
Av. 62
Calle 37
Parque Villuendas
Av. 60
Av. 58
Av. 56
Parque José Martí
Av. 54
REPARTO PUEBLO-NUEVO
Av. 52
Train Station

Parque 5 de Septiembre
7
7A
9A
11
Av. 50
Av. 48
13
15
17
Av. 46
Av. 44
19
21
23
25
27
29
31
33
35
Av. 50
Av. 48
43
45
47
49
Av. 42
Av. 46
Av. 40

Ensenada de Marsillán

Av. 44
Av. 42
Av. 40
Av. 38
Av. 36
Av. 34
7→ Av. 5 de Septiembre

Punta Majagua

REPARTO PUNTA GORDA
Av. 30
Av. 28
Av. 26

25
27
Av. 56
2
29
8
Parque José Martí
1
3 5
10
Av. 54
Av. 52
31

Punta Revienta Cordeles
Av. 22
Av. 20
Av. 18
Av. 16
Av. 14
9
Av. 12
Av. 10
Laguna del Cura

←6

Punta del Medio
Av. 8
Av. 6
Av. 4
H (Hospital)
Av. 2
5
Av. 0
11

① Parque José Martí
② Teatro Tomás Terry
③ Casa del Fundador
④ Punta Gorda
⑤ La Bodega de Valle
⑥ Castillo de Jagua
⑦ Jardín Botánico Soledad

Where to Stay & Dine

Casa Amistad **8**
Hostal Palacio Azul **9**
Hotel La Unión **10**
Palacio del Valle **11**
Villa Lagarto **12**

+ Hospital
✉ Post Office

0 ___ 1/4 mi
0 ___ 0.25 km

N

★ **Havana**
Cienfuegos○
CUBA

4 *Punta Gorda* **12**

Known as La Perla del Sur (the Southern Pearl), Cienfuegos is an uncharacteristically calm and inviting port. It wasn't until 1819, when a group of French colonists settled here, that the city began to grow and develop. French influence continued through most of its history, particularly throughout the 19th century when Cienfuegos was a major shipping point for sugar, tobacco, and coffee.

❶ Parque José Martí. This city hub, formerly the Plaza de Armas, is a broad park with a bandstand at its center and a little Arc of Triumph dating from 1902 at its western end. Surrounding the park are some of Cienfuegos' most interesting historical buildings. The 1918 **Palacio Ferrer** is the city's Casa de la Cultura. Check out the view from the rooftop cupola here. At the eastern end of the park, keep an eye out for the **Catedral de la Purísima Concepción,** a neoclassical church finished in 1870. The church features handsome stained-glass work imported from France. *Palacio Ferrer.* ☎ *43/51-9722. Admission CUC$0.50.*

❷ ★ Teatro Tomás Terry. On the north side of the park is the city theater, inaugurated in 1890. Stars such as Enrico Caruso, Sarah Bernhardt, and Anna Pavlova performed here. You can tour the wonderfully maintained facility during the day.

Punta Gorda.

Arc de Triomph, Parque José Martí.

The auditorium ceiling is magically painted with birds and flowers around its centerpiece. 🕐 *30 min. Parque José Martí.* ☎ *43/51-3361. www.azurina.cult.cu. Admission CUC$1. Daily 9am–6pm.*

❸ Casa del Fundador. Pause for an ice-cream and a drink under the big iron porch lamps at this small corner café. *Av 54 y 29, esq Parque. No phone. $.*

❹ ★ Punta Gorda. Out on the end of a long thin peninsula that juts into the Bay of Cienfuegos, is the historic old **Palacio del Valle,** an eclectic architectural masterpiece. The centerpiece here is the **Salón Comedor** (dining room), which dates to 1917 and tries to imitate the intricate Moorish stucco and

Beny Moré

Maximiliano Bartolomé Moré, better known as Beny Moré but most descriptively dubbed 'El Bárbaro del Ritmo' (The Rhythm Barbarian), is the pride of Cienfuegos. Born in the nearby hamlet of Santa Isabel de las Lajas on 24th August, 1919, Moré was the greatest Cuban singer and bandleader of his time. He sang and composed in a variety of genres, from mambo to *son* to *cha-cha-chá*. Tall and thin, with a velvet-smooth voice, Moré was the epitome of the debonair Cuban bandleader of the 1940s and 1950s. Although he never enjoyed the overseas success of Xavier Cugat or Pérez Prado, in Cuba Beny Moré is considered the king. His life and voice were recently immortalized in the 2006 movie, El Benny. His bronze statue stands on Cienfuegos' main thoroughfare, Prado.

Beny Moré statue.

tilework of Spain's Alhambra. Other rooms are done variously in baroque, neoclassical, and Gothic styling. It's now a restaurant (see below).

5 La Bodega de Valle. Descend beneath the Palacio del Valle for tapas at this pretty, authentic bar, decorated with tiles and dark wood. *Punta Gorda*. ☎ *43/55-1003 ext. 173*. *$–$$*.

6 ★ Castillo de Jagua. The Jagua castle, on the western flank of the narrow entrance to the harbor, was built between 1738 and 1745. Although the moat is dry, you still enter the castle by crossing the wooden drawbridge. Inside, there are basic exhibits and a mediocre state-run restaurant. Take the boat

from Calles 23 y 46 at 8am and 1pm, returning 10am and 3pm respectively (CUC$1 one-way). ☎ *43/9-6402*. *Admission CUC$1. Mon–Sat 9.30am–5pm, Sun 9.30am–1pm*.

7 ★ Jardín Botánico Soledad. This flourishing oasis was begun by US sugar magnate Edwin Atkins in 1900, and taken over by Harvard University in 1919. With more than 2,000 species of plants covering 90 hectares (222 acres), it is the most extensive botanical garden in Cuba. The grounds are beautiful to walk around, and there's usually good bird-watching, although everything tends to be overgrown and unkempt, and markings are sorely lacking. Located 17km (10 miles) east of downtown, on the road to Trinidad. *C/ Central 136, Pepito Tey*, ☎ *43/54-5334*. *Admission CUC$3. Daily 8am–4.30pm*.

Where to **Stay & Dine**

★ **Casa Amistad**   Run by the superfriendly and knowledgeable Armando and Leonor, this colonial home, a stone's throw from Parque José Martí, boasts a wonderful front living room, two rooms, and some hearty home-cooked food, including Leonor's famous chicken cooked in cola. A wrought-iron staircase leads to a sun terrace where you can enjoy cocktails at sunset. *Av. 56 no. 2927 e/ Calles 29 and 31.* ☎ *43/51-6143. casa mistad@correodecuba.cu. Two rooms. CUC$20–25 double. No credit cards.*

★ **Hostal Palacio Azul**   This newly restored waterfront building is excellent value, offering comfortable rooms out near the tip of Punta Gorda. Rooms in the 1920s building have high, decorated ceilings and beautiful tiled floors (c. 1921). A

Palacio del Valle.

grand marble staircase leads up to my favorite room, Dalia, a corner unit with a view of the Club Cienfuegos, the harbor, and the nightly sunset. *C/ 37 no. 1201, e/ Avs. 12 and 14.* ☎ *43/55-5828. www.hotel escubanacan.com. Seven rooms. CUC$60 double w/breakfast. MC, V.*

★★ **Hotel La Unión**   This handsome hotel, housed in a restored mint-green 1869 colonial mansion, is one of the nicest boutique hotels in the country. The inviting pool is located in an interior courtyard. *C/ 31 esq Av. 54.* ☎ *43/55-1020. www. hotelescubanacan.com. 49 rooms. CUC$100 double w/breakfast. MC, V.*

★ **Palacio del Valle** CONTINENTAL/SEAFOOD   The food is not nearly as spectacular as the setting, but the luxurious and ornate surroundings just about make up for it. Music and entertainment are provided by the charismatic María del Carmen Iznaga Guillén, the niece of the great Cuban poet Nicolás Guillén. My favorite draw here is the rooftop bar, with its fabulous views over the harbor and surrounding mountains. *C/ 37 (Prado) and Av. 0, Punta Gorda.* ☎ *43/55-1003. Reservations recommended in high season. Mains CUC$9–25. No credit cards. Daily 10am–midnight.*

Villa Lagarto   Run by the very friendly Tony and Maylin, this Punta Gorda property has two breezy, comfortable top-floor rooms, a seawater pool, and a garden overlooking the sea right at the tip of the peninsula. Cocktails at sunset overlooking the waves lapping the shore are a must. *C/ 35 no. 4B.* ☎ *43/51-9966. villalagarto_16@yahoo.com. Two rooms. CUC$20–25 double. No credit cards.*

Matanzas

1 Plaza de la Vigía & Parque de la Libertad
2 Teatro Sauto
3 Museo Farmacéutico
4 Castillo de San Severino
5 Cuevas de Bellamar
6 Yumurí Valley

Where to Stay, Drink & Dine

Café Atenas **7**
Casa Alma **8**
Hostal Azul **9**

Bahía de Matanzas

Río Yumurí

Puente de la Concordia

Parque de la Libertad

Plaza de la Vigía

67 (Santa Isabel)
71 (Salamanca)
73 (Velarde)
75 (Daoíz)
77 (Maceo)

260 (San Isidro)

49
53
55
57
63 (Isabel)
65
67
69
71

270
272
276
278

Contreras (Bonifacio Byrne)
José J. Milanés

CUBA
Havana
○ Matanzas

0   1/4 mil
0   0.25 km

Matanzas is a city of many names: City of Bridges, City of Rivers, and the Venice of Cuba. They all refer to the fact that the city is divided by two major rivers. Due to its slow pace and laid-back nature, Matanzas is also sometimes called Cuba's Sleeping Beauty. However, the city is most proud of its moniker as the Athens of Cuba, a name reflecting Matanzas's important cultural history. The first danzón, a languid and lyrical original dance and musical form, was originally composed and played in Matanzas in 1879 by native son Miguel Failde, and Matanzas has a rich legacy of poets, writers, painters, and musicians.

❶ Plaza de la Vigía & Parque de la Libertad. These two small plazas anchor the social and cultural life of Matanzas. Both are within five blocks of each other in the center. Parque de la Libertad is dominated by a fine statue of José Martí and surrounded by handsome buildings, including the proud and ornate former Casino Español.

❷ ★ Teatro Sauto. This neoclassical theater dominates the Plaza de la Vigía. Completed in 1863, it was the design of Italian architect and artist Daniel Dal'Aglio, who also painted the frescoes that adorn the ceiling. Dance, theater, and classical music performances are still held in the surrounds of its stunning interior, and it's worth checking to see whether anything's playing while

The decorative interior of Teatro Sauto.

you're in town (Tues–Sun). Otherwise, take a guided tour of the theater and foyer. 🕐 *30 min. Plaza de la Vigía.* ☎ *45/24-2721. Tour CUC$2. Daily 9am–5pm.*

Plaza de la Vigía.

A Side Trip to Cárdenas

Cárdenas lies 18km (11 miles) southeast of Varadero and is known as Cuba's 'Ciudad Bandera' (Flag City). It was here, in 1850, that the national flag was first flown. Fronting the diminutive **Parque Colón** is the **Catedral de la Concepción Inmaculada,** famous for its stained glass. The town's market, **Plaza Molokoff,** is housed in an L-shaped iron building, topped with a high ornate dome. Out by the water's edge is the **Arrechabala Rum Factory,** where the Havana Club brand was born and where present-day Varadero and Buccanero rums are made. Tours run daily, at 9am and 4pm (CUC\$2). Elián Gonzalez, the boy who became the center of an international custody dispute in late 1999 when he washed up near Miami, lives in town. The **Museo Batalla de Ideas** (Museum of the Ideological Battle) (☎ 45/52-3990) is housed in a restored building, and features exhibits honoring the child celebrity, alongside numerous displays documenting Cuba's battles. Admission is CUC\$1, and it's open Monday to Saturday from 9am to 6pm and Sunday 9am to 1pm.

❸ ★ **Museo Farmacéutico.**
Seemingly little has changed here since its founding in 1882 by the French pharmacist Ernesto Troilet. Porcelain jars of potions and elixirs are stacked high in beautiful floor-to-ceiling wood cabinets. ⏱ *1 hr. C/ 83 no. 4951, Plaza de la Libertad.* ☎ *45/24-3179. Admission CUC\$3. Mon–Sat 10am–5pm, Sun 10am–2pm.*

❹ **Castillo de San Severino.**
Out on the northern edge of the bay, this small fort, built in 1693, served as a line of defense, slave-trading post, and long-standing prison. It's been restored and is definitely worth a visit, if only for the view of Matanzas Bay. ⏱ *1 hr. Av del Muelle. Admission CUC\$2. Mon–Sat 9am–5pm, Sun 9am–1pm.*

❺ ★ **kids Cuevas de Bellamar.**
On the outskirts of the city is a cave complex containing nearly 3km (2 miles) of galleries and passageways, with intricate stalactite and stalagmite formations, indigenous pictographs, and several underground streams and rivers. You can tour the first kilometer or so of caves. This section is lit, and so no equipment or flashlights are needed. ⏱ *2 hrs. Finca La Alcancia, 5km (3 miles) southeast of Matanzas, off a well-marked access road.* ☎ *45/26-1683. Admission CUC\$5 including guide. Daily 9.30am–4.15pm.*

❻ ★ **Yumurí Valley.** At 108m (360 feet) high, the Bacuanayagua Bridge is the highest in Cuba. It spans the beautiful Yumurí Valley, which is thick with palm trees at varying elevations. The lush vista is breathtaking. A rugged side road leads off the highway if you want to explore this largely undeveloped valley. 7km (4½ miles) west of Matanzas, on the Via Blanca from Havana.

Where to **Stay & Dine**

Café Atenas   Facing the Teatro Sauto, this simple café serving up snacks is the most happening place in town. Ambience is easygoing and there's comfortable seating both indoors and out on a cool patio. *C/ Magdalena and C/ Milanés, Plaza de la Vigía.* ☎ *45/25-3493. Daily noon–midnight.*

★ **Casa Alma**   This late 19th-century home with huge rooms, original decorative floor tiles, and striking *mediopuntos* offers the best accommodation (and food) in town. There are two en suite rooms at the (quieter) back of the house, plus air conditioning, a fan, and a refrigerator. *C/ Milanés (C/ 83) 29008 e/ 290 y 292.* ☎ *45-242449. Two rooms. CUC\$20–25 double. No credit cards.*

Casa Alma.

Hostal Azul   Two doors down from Casa Alma is this lovely Spanish colonial home painted in blue and decorated with multiple patterned original floor tiles. There's a covered porch at the back and a sun-lit patio. The two second-floor rooms face the patio. *C/ Milanés (C/ 83) 29012 e/ 290 y 292.* ☎ *45-242449. Two rooms. CUC\$20–25 double. No credit cards.*

Matanzas' Nightlife

Younger sister to the venerable Tropicana in Havana, **Tropicana Matanzas** (☎ 45/26-5380), Autopista del Sur Km 4.5, provides the classic cabaret experience to thousands of tourists who never venture far from Varadero. Like its famous sibling, this is a large open-air theater with extravagant nightly performances. Artistic direction is shared between the two venues: scantily clad showgirls and dancers seamlessly weave together a series of different numbers. Costumes are tight-fitting, garish, and often feature gravity-defying headgear. The spectacle covers most of the bases of popular Cuban show and dance music, from *son* to bolero to *danzón* to salsa, with a bit of Afro-Cuban religious music thrown into the mix. The 90-minute show starts around 10.30pm each night. Afterwards, dance the night away at the adjoining dance club. Every Varadero tour agency can book you a night at the Tropicana Matanzas; tickets are CUC\$35. You get your money back if there's a rainout.

Remedios

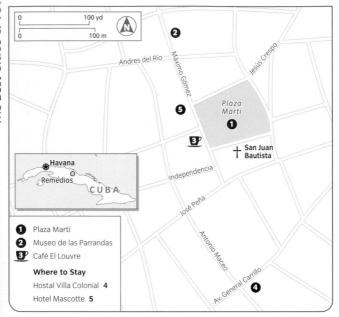

0 — 100 yd
0 — 100 m

Andres del Rio

Máximo Gómez

Jesús Crespo

Plaza Martí ❶

† San Juan Bautista

❺

☕❸

Independencia

José Peña

Antonio Maceo

Av. General Carrillo ❹

❷

Havana
Remedios
CUBA

❶ Plaza Martí
❷ Museo de las Parrandas
☕❸ Café El Louvre

Where to Stay
Hostal Villa Colonial **4**
Hotel Mascotte **5**

The tiny old city of Remedios, near the northern coast, is one of Cuba's colonial highlights. It was founded as an eighth villa in 1515 by Vasco Porcallo de Figueroa. The Spaniards tried to coerce locals to move to Santa Clara and leave their rich farms behind by convincing them that there were many demons in Remedios. Many refused to leave. The town grew rich on the back of sugar in the 19th century, evidenced by many of the smart colonial buildings lining the streets of the city center. Remedios is 45km (28 miles) northeast of Santa Clara on a direct two-lane highway. There's not a whole lot to see in Remedios, but that's part of its charm; it's well known for its Christmas Eve fiesta, Las Parrandas.

❶ ★★ **Plaza Martí.** This small square sits at the colonial center of Remedios, watched over by the **Iglesia de San Juan Bautista,** with its stunning baroque-style altar covered in 22-karat gold and a celebrated pregnant Madonna statue. 🕐 *30 min. Plaza Mayor. Free admission. Mon–Fri 9am–noon, 2–5pm, Sat 2–5pm.*

❷ **Museo de las Parrandas.** For several weeks at the end of each year, Remedios becomes the site of one of Cuba's great street parties and religious carnivals, **Las Parrandas.** The infectious revelry keeps things lively throughout the holiday season. Everything culminates on Christmas Eve in an orgy of drums, floats, and fireworks. The

Plaza Martí.

whole thing allegedly began in 1820, when the local priest sent some altar boys out to bang on pots and pans and scare parishioners into the midnight Advent Masses. It later evolved into a sort of battle of the bands and fireworks between two sections of the small town. Today, the festivities drag out over the weeks leading up to Christmas Eve, and have even spread into neighboring hamlets. Still, Plaza Martí in Remedios is the place to be, and the night to be there is 24 December. Be prepared to stay up late, and bring some ear protection.

If you're not here at Christmas, pop in to this museum where you can get an idea of the pageantry by examining the small display of photos, costumes, and floats. ⏱ *30 min. C/ Máximo Gómez 71. Admission CUC$1. Tues–Sat 9am–noon, 1–6pm, Sun 9am–1pm.*

3 Café El Louvre. An atmospheric café with big blue wooden doors set on a corner facing the town's central plaza and church. Sit on tables on the pavement or prop up the long wooden bar counter. Besides casas and the reopened Hotel Mascotte, this is the only eatery in town. *Plaza Martí.* ☎ *42/39-5639. $.*

Where to **Stay**

★ **Hostal Villa Colonial**   This lovely colonial house has a gorgeous front room with wonderful furniture and original flower-design floor tiling. There are two en suite rooms in the house—one with bronze antique bedsteads and decorative mother of pearl panels. Owners Frank and Arelys are extremely helpful. *C/ Antonio Maceo 43 e/ Av General Carrillo and Fe de Valle.* ☎ *42/39-6274. www.cubavillacolonial.com. Two rooms. CUC$ 20–25 double. No credit cards.*

Hotel Mascotte   The only hotel in Remedios at the moment is this quaint and modest boutique hotel with a lovely aspect facing the central park. It has undergone a complete renovation and has been transformed into a Hoteles E brand hotel by Cubanacán. *C/ Máximo Gómez 114, e/ C/ Margal and Av del Río.* ☎ *42/39-5144. www.hoteles cubanacan.com. 10 rooms. CUC$60 double. MC, V.*

Sancti **Spíritus**

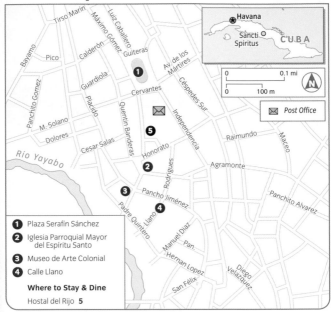

1 Plaza Serafín Sánchez
2 Iglesia Parroquial Mayor
   del Espíritu Santo
3 Museo de Arte Colonial
4 Calle Llano

Where to Stay & Dine
Hostal del Rijo 5

Sancti Spíritus, perched on the banks of the Río Yayabo, is a warren of corkscrew streets lined with fine, if weathered, colonial homes. The old town was one of the original seven *villas* founded by conquistador Velázquez in the early 16th century. Today, it's a small provincial capital with an unassuming, lived-in feel.

1 Plaza Serafín Sánchez. The main public square with a handful of fine colonial buildings is dominated by the **Biblioteca Provincial Rubén Martínez,** an early-20th-century library that looks more like an opera house.

2 ★ Iglesia Parroquial Mayor del Espíritu Santo. One of the best-preserved colonial churches in Cuba, this small, faded-blue church has a tall bell tower and austere construction that dates from 1680.

The church's massive ceiling beams are impressive, as is the blue-and-yellow painted nave. ⏱ *10 min. Jesús Menéndez e/ Honorato and Agramonte. No phone. Free admission. Tues–Sat 9–11am, 2–5pm.*

3 ★★ Museo de Arte Colonial. This opulent former palatial mansion was home to one of Cuba's elite families, the Valle-Iznaga clan. Though the family obviously kept an impressive collection of Limoges porcelain, French gilded mirrors,

Italian marble tables, and Baccarat crystal chandeliers here, this wasn't their primary residence. The three bedrooms are decorated in grand style, with handmade lace, embroidered sheets, and hand-painted glass. Note the gorgeous and very Cuban leather *sillón fumador* (smoking chair). In the tearoom is the family seal. ⏱ *45 min. C/ Plácido 74 esq Jesús Menéndez.* ☎ *41/32-5455. Admission CUC$2. Tues–Sat 9.30am– 5pm, Sun 8am–noon.*

④ ★ Calle Llano. This is the most atmospheric street in Sancti Spíritus, a bent-elbow cobblestone alleyway (one of the only remaining stone streets in town) of pastel-colored and tiled-roof houses where children play and daily life unfolds.

Museo de Arte Colonial.

Where to **Stay & Dine**

★★ Hostal del Rijo This handsomely restored, light-blue colonial mansion is part of a growing trend in elegant boutique hotels, and best of all, it's a steal. It exudes colonial character and charm with its huge rooms and balconies. The two-story structure is built around a lovely patio with a fountain, where you can find the hotel's excellent restaurant, whose chef is more adventurous than most in Cuba. *C/ Honorato del Castillo 12.* ☎ *41/32-8588. www. hotelescubanacan.com. 16 rooms. CUC$49 double. Restaurant: mains CUC$3.50–18. MC, V. Daily 7am– 11pm.*

Hostal del Rijo restaurant.

Santa **Clara**

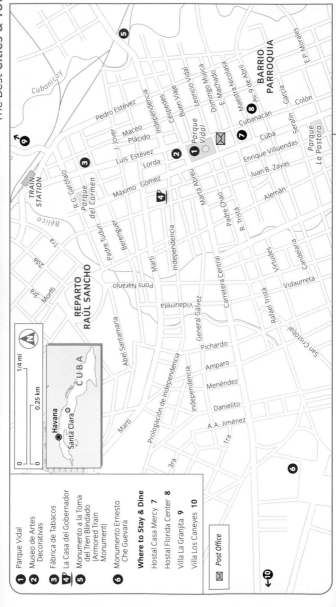

1 Parque Vidal
2 Museo de Artes Decorativas
3 Fábrica de Tabacos
4 La Casa del Gobernador
5 Monumento a la Toma del Tren Blindado (Armored Train Monument)
6 Monumento Ernesto Che Guevara

Where to Stay & Dine

Hostal Casa Mercy **7**
Hostal Florida Center **8**
Villa La Granjita **9**
Villa Los Caneyes **10**

Post Office

This quiet university town was founded in 1689 by settlers from Remedios looking for a site inland less vulnerable to pirate attack. It's home to one of Cuba's principal colleges, la Universidad Central de las Villas (Las Villas Central University), and played an important role in both the independence and revolutionary wars. Thanks to the latter, Santa Clara is known as 'Che Guevara's City.' Today, it's also home to several industrial factories, the legacy of Guevara's tenure as Minister of Industry and his special relationship with this city; his mausoleum sits in the Plaza de la Revolución. The city is strategically located on the island's spine, right on the main highway and train lines, and is the capital of Villa Clara province.

1 **Parque Vidal.** This park is the heart of the city. The double-wide streets ringing the park are pedestrian-only and often crowded with locals and lovers strolling in leisurely circles. The **Teatro La Caridad** facing the park is an ornate 19th-century theater, modeled after the Paris Opera, and often features concerts and shows. It's worth a quick tour during the day, although it's closed and undergoing restoration at the time of writing. *Parque Vidal.* ☎ *42/20-5548. Admission CUC$1.*

2 **Museo de Artes Decorativas.** This 18th-century house, last owned by a woman named Clara Cartas, now houses a wonderful collection of furnishings. The house is stuffed full of Baccarat crystal and chandeliers, including a 'spaghetti' chandelier. Its other unusual items include a rocking chair with a carved protruding face at its tip to stop a nanny from falling asleep, and a wall plate imprinted with the image of the Crystal Palace in London. ⏲ *30 min. Parque Vidal.* ☎ *42/20-5368. Admission CUC$2. Mon–Thurs 9am–noon, Fri 1–6pm, Sat 1–6pm, 7–10pm, Sun 6–10pm.*

3 ★ **Fábrica de Tabacos.** This cigar factory occupies a full city block and produces high-quality Montecristo, Partagás, Romeo y Julieta, Punch, and Robaina cigars.

Across the street, there's a well-stocked shop, **La Casa del Tabaco,**

Ron y Café La Veguita, C/ Maceo 176-A (☎ 42/20-8952). The cigar sommelier, Marilin Morales Bauta, is quite charming and one of the premier experts in the field. *C/ Maceo 181.* ☎ *42/20-2211. Mon–Fri 9–11am, 1–3pm. 20-min guided tour costs CUC$3 per person; the ticket must be bought at one of the three tour agencies in town. Shop: Mon–Sat 9am–5pm.*

4 **La Casa del Gobernador.** Tables are spread around a couple of rooms and an open-air interior courtyard of this old colonial home facing the town's pedestrianized boulevard. *C/ Zayas esq Independencia.* ☎ *42/20-2273; closed Mon. $.*

Teatro La Caridad.

Santa Clara's Nightlife

With an artsy bohemian vibe, Club Mejunje, C/ Marta Abreu 12 (☎ 42/28-2572) is probably my favorite spot, featuring regular concerts, poetry readings, gay night on Saturday, and theater pieces put on in the brick-walled, open-air courtyard. Cover is CUC$2. **Bar La Marquesina,** opposite the Teatro de la Caridad on Máximo Gómez, draws locals and tourists to nightly live music; there's always a friendly buzz.

⑤ Monumento a la Toma del Tren Blindado (Armored Train Monument). A popular revolutionary landmark is this derailed train at Carretera Camajuani and the train line. It's a small park built around the spot where Che Guevara and his soldiers derailed an armored train during the critical battles for control of Santa Clara in 1958. In addition to the five cars and some sculptures, there's a tiny museum in this pleasant open-air park. ⏱ *20 min. No phone. Admission CUC$1. Mon–Sat 9am–5.30pm.*

⑥ ★ Monumento Ernesto Che Guevara. Che Guevara's mausoleum features a huge sculpture of the revolutionary hero, overlooking a vast plaza where massive demonstrations and music concerts are often held. Underneath the statue is a museum with exhibits detailing the life and exploits of 'El Che.' The adjoining mausoleum holds Guevara's remains, as well as the tombstones (and some of the remains) of 37 other revolutionary fighters killed alongside Guevara in Bolivia. A new graveyard, containing the remains of other fighters, is due to open behind the mausoleum. ⏱ *45 min– 1 hr. Plaza de la Revolución Che Guevara.* ☎ *42/20-5878. Free admission. Tues–Sun 9am–5.30pm. No cameras or video cameras allowed.*

Monumento Ernesto Che Guevara.

Where to **Stay & Dine**

Hostal Casa Mercy This central, modern house with an internal patio and a sun terrace, is run by the friendly Mercedes and Omelio. Casa Mercy offers two bright second-floor rooms, a cocktail menu, and a rare find in Cuba—a book exchange. *C/ E Machado (San Cristóbal) 4 e/ Cuba and Colón.* ☎ *42/21-6941. isel@uclv. edu.cu. Two rooms. CUC$25 double. No credit cards.*

★★ Hostal Florida Center
This gorgeous 1876 colonial house is full of interesting historic furniture and is blessed with a garden full of flourishing plants and a welcoming host, Angel. He also serves up some of the best food in Cuba (see next entry for details of the restaurant). The breakfast is, without doubt, the most elaborate served in any private home in the country. One of the en suite rooms is artfully decorated in colonial style; the other features art-deco furniture.

The owner has helped open another charming colonial home down the road: **Hostal Alba.** *C/ Maestra Nicolasa (Candelaria) 56, e/ Colón and Maceo.* ☎ *42/20-8161. Two rooms. CUC$25 double. No credit cards.*

★★ Hostal Florida Center
COMIDA CRIOLLA Reservations are required. *C/ Maestra Nicolasa (Candelaria) 56, e/ Colón and Maceo.* ☎ *42/20-8161. Mains CUC$8–10. No credit cards. Lunch & dinner daily.*

Villa La Granjita Octagonal, one and two-story, thatched-roof buildings scattered around rural grounds make this quiet hotel, 4 km (2½ miles) from the center, a good

Hostal Florida Center.

choice. Rooms are on the small side, but are comfortable and most have balconies; some have views toward the inviting pool. The hotel also has green credentials: solar power heats the water. *Carretera a Maleza Km 2.5.* ☎ *42/21-8190. www.hoteles cubanacan.com. 65 rooms. CUC$65–72 double w/breakfast. MC, V.*

★ **Villa Los Caneyes** Built to resemble a Taino Indian village, this mini-resort is the most comfortable hotel in Santa Clara. Most of the rooms are housed in large, round, six-unit structures or individual bungalows. All are clean and roomy. The grounds are planted with tall trees and flowering plants, and there's good bird-watching all around. It's located about 2 km (1 mile) from downtown. *Av. de los Eucaliptos and Circunvalación.* ☎ *42/21-8140. www.hotelescubanacan.com. 96 rooms. CUC$65–72 double w/breakfast. MC, V.*

Santiago de **Cuba**

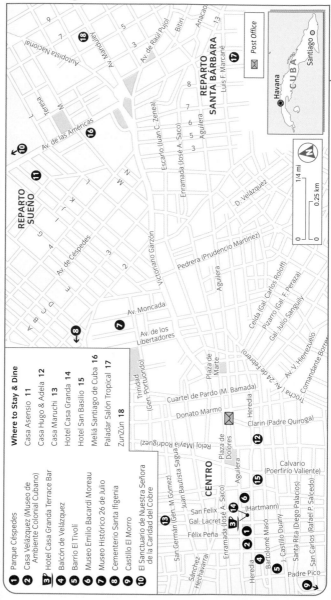

Where to Stay & Dine

Casa Asensio **11**
Casa Hugo & Adela **12**
Casa Maruchi **13**
Hotel Casa Granda **14**
Hotel San Basilio **15**
Meliá Santiago de Cuba **16**
Paladar Salón Tropical **17**
ZunZún **18**

1 Parque Céspedes
2 Casa Velázquez (Museo de Ambiente Colonial Cubano)
3 Hotel Casa Granda Terrace Bar
4 Balcón de Velázquez
5 Barrio El Tívoli
6 Museo Emilio Bacardí Moreau
7 Museo Histórico 26 de Julio
8 Cementerio Santa Ifigenia
9 Castillo El Morro
10 El Sanctuario de Nuestra Señora de la Caridad del Cobre

REPARTO SUEÑO

REPARTO SANTA BÁRBARA

CENTRO

⊠ Post Office

CUBA

Havana

Santiago

0   1/4 mi
0   0.25 km

Vibrant, tropical, and often sweltering, Cuba's second-largest city is the country's liveliest cultural showpiece outside Havana. Santiago, with a unique history and rhythms all its own, has produced some of Cuba's greatest contemporary musicians as well as several of its most stalwart revolutionaries. It has the largest Afro-Cuban population in Cuba and a resolutely Afro-Caribbean feel that distinguishes it from the rest of Cuba.

❶ ★ Parque Céspedes. A gathering spot for Santiagueros, the park's surrounds are a menagerie of eclectic architecture. Its benches, tall trees, and gas lamps are ringed by colonial, 19th-century, and modern structures, including the mansion of Diego Velázquez, as well as the handsome Town Hall, the cathedral, and the city's oldest hotel, Casa Granda. The **Town Hall,** a large white building with blue wooden grilles on the north side of the square, was originally built in 1515. It was greatly renovated in the 1950s after an earthquake, but has retained its elegant colonial lines, balcony, and patio. Fidel Castro addressed the masses here on 1 January, 1959, after the rebel army had taken the city and announced the triumph of La Revolución. Across the park, the 19th-century **Catedral de Nuestra Señora de la Asunción** is an ornate basilica with twin towers—one of several churches to occupy the site since 1522. The frescoes on the arches and dome of the interior have been magnificently restored. ⏱ 25 min. Free admission. Tues–Sat 8am–12.30pm, 5–7.30pm, Sun 8–11am, 5–6.30pm.

❷ ★★ Casa Velázquez (Museo de Ambiente Colonial Cubano). The mansion (c. 1516) once belonged t o conquistador Diego Velázquez. The house has a notable Moorish influence, with a wonderful carved cedar ceiling. You can marvel at some splendid pieces of international furniture. ⏱ 1 hr.

Town Hall, Parque Céspedes.

C/ Félix Peña 612 esq Aguilera. ☎ 22/65-2652. Admission CUC$2. Sat–Thurs 9am–1pm, 2–5pm, Fri 2–5pm.

❸ Hotel Casa Granda Terrace Bar. A great spot for people-watching over Parque Céspedes, this convivial terrace bar is always hopping, with a good mix of foreigners and Cubans. C/ Heredia 201 e/ General Lacret and San Félix. ☎ 22/65-3021. $.

❹ Balcón de Velázquez. Stop here and look out over the city's red-tile rooftops as it slopes down

Hotel Casa Granda Terrace bar.

to the Bay of Santiago. *C/ Heredia esq C/ Corona.*

5 Barrio El Tívolí. This charming, hilly neighborhood was once the most fashionable place to live in Santiago. Today, it's a relaxed place of steep streets, weathered and decrepit wooden houses, and a good place to wander. The famous **Padre Pico steps** are named after a Santiaguero priest who aided the city's poor. Take the steps up to the **Museo de la Lucha Clandestina** (Museum of the Underground Struggle), housed in a handsome 18th-century mansion. Inside, exhibits relate to the November 1956 attack on this former police headquarters, led by rebel leader Frank País, executed by the army. ⏱ *30 min. General Rabí 1 e/ Santa Rita and San Carlos.* ☎ *22/62-4689. Admission CUC$1. Tues–Sun 9am–5pm.*

6 ★ Museo Emilio Bacardi Moreau. Begun by Emilio Bacardi, the son of the founder of the rum dynasty, in 1899, this personal collection constituted one of the first museums in Cuba. Today, it's an eclectic art and historical assembly. There's an extensive array of armaments and a peculiar coffin-shaped

torpedo used by the Mambíses. Bacardí also collected personal items belonging to national heroes, including those of Antonio Maceo and Carlos Manuel de Céspedes. ⏱ *1 hr. C/ Pío Rosado esq Aguilera.* ☎ *22/62-8402. Admission CUC$2. Mon noon–4.15pm, Tues–Sat 9–11.45am, 1–4.15pm, Sun 9am–noon.*

7 ★ Museo Histórico 26 de Julio. The ocher-colored exterior of the Moncada barracks is still pock-marked with bullet holes, a reminder of July 1953 when Fidel Castro and a band of idealistic rebels launched an assault on the barracks, with the intention of stealing arms and jump-starting a revolution. Today, the Art Deco–style barracks house a museum focused on that day and the revolutionary struggle. ⏱ *1 hr. C/ Trinidad esq Moncada.* ☎ *22/66-1157. Admission CUC$2. Tues–Sat 9.30am–5.15pm, Sun 9.15am–12.30pm.*

8 ★★ Cementerio Santa Ifigenia. Dating from 1868, this city of the dead includes several spectacular mausoleums. By far the most

Padre Pico steps.

Santiago Spirit

Founded in 1515, Santiago was one of the first of seven towns in Cuba, and was the Spanish colony's capital until 1553. Diego Velázquez, the founder of the original seven villas, built his mansion here (see ➋). After the 1791 revolution in Haiti, a large number of French coffee plantation owners fled with their African slaves and made their way to Santiago. Black Haitian workers followed, as did large contingencies of West African slaves, sold to work on the plantations. This rich heritage comes alive during the famous Carnival celebrations in July. Afro-Cuban religious traditions, including Santería, have their strongest hold here.

famous is that of José Martí, a massive stone and marble circular structure built in 1951. Don't miss the changing of the guard ceremony. In addition to Marti, the remains of Emilio Bacardí, Carlos Manuel de Céspedes, and musician Compay Segundo lie here. ◷ *1 hr. Calzada Crombet.* ☎ *22/63-2723. Admission CUC$1. Daily 7am–6pm.*

➒ ★★ kids **Castillo El Morro.** Guarding the entrance to the Bahía de Santiago, this fortress is built atop a rocky promontory and entered across a drawbridge. It was engineered in 1638 to protect against pirate attacks. The site has magnificent views of the Caribbean coastline. Inside the fortress is a sparse museum detailing the history of piracy, El Morro, and Santiago de Cuba. One room contains artifacts related to the 1898 Spanish-American War—its principal naval battles were fought in the Bay of Santiago. A daily ceremony, Puesta del Sol, takes place at sunset. Youngsters dressed as *mambises* (members of the Cuban rebel army) lower the flag and fire the ancient (c. 1805) Spanish cannon. ◷ *1 hr. Bahía de Santiago.* ☎ *22/69-1569. Admission CUC$4. Daily 9am–8pm.*

➓ **El Sanctuario de Nuestra Señora de la Caridad del Cobre.** This triple-domed church, built in 1927, is the most important shrine in Cuba and photogenically framed by green forest. The faithful come from across Cuba on pilgrimages to pay their respects to (and ask for protection from) a black Madonna, the Virgen de la Caridad (Virgin of Charity). She is nothing less than the protectress of Cuba. The annual pilgrimage is on 12 September. ◷ *45 min. Free admission. Daily 6am–6.30pm.*

Castillo El Morro.

Where to **Stay & Dine**

Casa Maruchi.

★ **Casa Asensio**   This fine house boasts a huge upstairs apartment with an even larger, private rooftop terrace. There's an independent entrance, separate kitchen, large, comfortable bed, and good-size bathroom. *C/ J no. 306 e/ C/ 6 and Av. de las Américas, Reparto Sueño.* ☎ *22/62-4600. manuel@medired. scu.sld.cu. One room. CUC$25 double. No credit cards.*

★ **Casa Hugo & Adela**   High above the hubbub below, and featuring an expansive, private corner terrace with incredible views of Santiago all the way to the bay, this place rents one large third-floor room with an independent entrance. The owners are very friendly and speak English. *C/ San Basilio (Bartolomé Masó) 501 esq Reloj.* ☎ *22/62-6359. One room. CUC$25–30 double. No credit cards.*

★ **Casa Maruchi**   This is a lovely colonial house with a wonderful patio stuffed with orchids and other plants. Two chic, comfortable rooms with exposed brickwork, Spanish colonial furniture, lace bedspreads, and candlesticks are off the patio.

C/ Hartmann (San Félix) 357 e/Trinidad and San Germán. ☎ *22/62-0767. maruchi@infomeil.com. Two rooms. CUC$20–25. No credit cards.*

★ **Hotel Casa Granda**   A large, elegant building right on Parque Céspedes, this classic Santiago hotel is a city landmark. Best known for its terrace bar with live music and its roof garden with great views over the cathedral and Santiago, the Casa Granda is one of the best places to stay in the city. *C/ Heredia 201 e/ San Félix and General Lacret.* ☎ *22/65-3021. www.gran-caribe. com. 58 units. CUC$84–110 double w/breakfast. MC, V.*

★ **Hotel San Basilio**   This little hotel, painted in olive green, is in a beautifully restored old home in the heart of downtown and now operates under the boutique Hoteles E brand. The rooms are charming and attractively decorated. *C/ Basilio 403 e/ Calvario and Carniceria.* ☎ *22/65-1702. www.hotelescubanacan.com. Eight rooms. CUC$60 double w/ breakfast. MC, V.*

Hotel San Basilio.

Santiago Nightlife

More cramped and intimate than the touristy Casa de la Trova, the superb **Casa de las Tradiciones** in Tívoli, C/ Rabí 154 (☎ 22/65-3892), is loaded with character. Cover is CUC$1. The legendary **Casa de la Trova,** C/ Heredia 206 e/ San Félix and San Pedro (☎ 22/65-2689) is the greatest of the country's Casas de la Trova, with live music in the afternoons and evenings, but evening sessions are touristy—the only Cubans listening to the music appear to be *jineteros.* Cover is CUC$1–10. The **Patio de ARTex,** C/ Heredia 304 e/ Pío Rosado and Porfirio Valiente (☎ 22/65-4814), showcases live Cuban music every afternoon and night. The cover of CUC$2 applies at night only. The **Patio de los Dos Abuelos,** C/ Pérez Carbó 5, across from Plaza de Marte (☎ 22/62-3302), is a good spot to listen to boleros and *filin* (feelin', a musical genre), daily from 10am to 2am (cover CUC$2 at night). Santiago also has its own **Tropicana** (Autopista Nacional, Km 1.5, north of the city; ☎ 22/64-2579; CUC$35.) The standout attraction, however, is the **Ballet Folklórico Cutumba,** an Afro-Cuban dance group: performances are energetic, colorful, riveting, and absorbing. While its normal venue undergoes restoration, performers can be found at the former Cine Galaxia, C/ Trocha esq Santa Ursula Av V. Hierrezuelo (www.cubanfolkloricdance.com/cutumba.php), rehearsing Tuesdays to Friday 9am–1pm.

★ Meliá Santiago de Cuba

A bright-red postmodern high-rise, Santiago's largest hotel has loads of facilities and services, including the best outdoor pool in the city. It sits out of the historic center, however, and is thus inconvenient for the majority of sightseeing. *Av. de las Américas esq Calle M, Reparto Sueño.* ☎ *22/68-7070. www.solmelia cuba.com. 302 rooms. CUC$93–113 double w/breakfast. MC, V.*

★ Paladar Salón Tropical

CRIOLLA One of the most elegant paladares in Cuba, this attractively decorated establishment also has a terrific, breezy, plant-covered terrace. Its own popularity has overwhelmed it, however, and service can be glacially slow at times. Depending upon what is available, the menu might offer a smorgasbord of options, including chicken soup, shish kabobs, grilled fish, mixed grill, or barbecued chicken. *C/ Luis Fernández Marcané 310 Altos e/ C/ 9 and 10, Reparto Santa Bárbara.* ☎ *22/64-1161. Mains CUC$4–7.50. No credit cards. Daily noon–11pm.*

★★ ZunZún *CRIOLLA* This elegant and upscale restaurant occupies a handsome 1940s house in the Vista Alegre neighborhood. It has four private salons for intimate dining, and a couple of tables on a broad front veranda, which are my favorites. It's especially good for seafood, such as a delicious mixed grill of fish and shellfish; medallions of lobster, shellfish, and shrimp; and garlic shrimp. *Av. Manduley 159, Reparto Vista Alegre.* ☎ *22/64-1528. Mains CUC$6–21. No credit cards. Daily noon–10pm.*

Trinidad

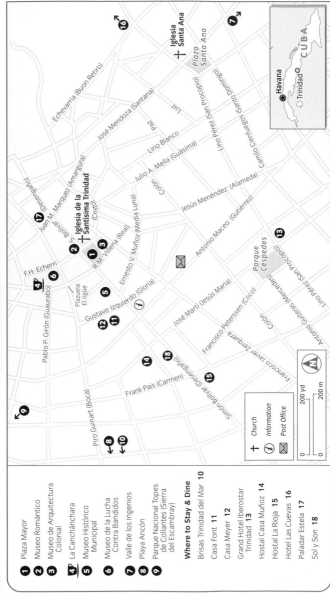

❶ Plaza Mayor
❷ Museo Romántico
❸ Museo de Arquitectura Colonial
❹ La Canchánchara
❺ Museo Histórico Municipal
❻ Museo de la Lucha Contra Bandidos
❼ Valle de los Ingenios
❽ Playa Ancón
❾ Parque Nacional Topes de Collantes (Sierra del Escambray)

Where to Stay & Dine

Brisas Trinidad del Mar **10**
Casa Font **11**
Casa Meyer **12**
Grand Hotel Iberostar Trinidad **13**
Hostal Casa Muñoz **14**
Hostal La Rioja **15**
Hotel Las Cuevas **16**
Paladar Estela **17**
Sol y Son **18**

✝ Church
ⓘ Information
☒ Post Office

Tiny Trinidad is one of the finest colonial towns in the Americas. A few square blocks of cobblestone streets, pretty pastel-colored 18th- and 19th-century houses, palaces, and plazas, Trinidad's colonial-era core can be toured in just a few hours. However, its serenity is so soothing that many visitors are coaxed into much longer stays. Magically frozen in time and tastefully scruffy where it needs to be, the city has streets that are more populated by horse-drawn carts than automobile traffic. Old folks still crouch by windows, behind elegant wrought-iron grilles, to peer out at passersby.

❶ ★★★ **Plaza Mayor.** The neo-baroque, 19th-century Plaza Mayor, elaborately adorned with serene sitting areas, statuary, towering palm trees, and gardens enclosed by white wrought-iron fences, is one of Cuba's perfect plazas. On the northeast corner is the cathedral, Iglesia de la Santísima Trinidad, which most locals refer to as La Parroquial Mayor. Completed in 1892, it replaced the original 17th-century church destroyed by a hurricane in 1812. The new construction, completed at the end of the 19th century, is rather simple on the outside, but the restored interior reveals a Gothic vaulted ceiling and nearly a dozen attractive carved altars. *Cathedral: No phone. Free admission. Mon–Sat 10.30am–1pm. Mass. Sat 4pm, Sun 9am.*

❷ ★★ **Museo Romántico.** The most evocative reminder of Trinidad's glory days is the lovingly restored **Palacio Brunet.** This colonial mansion dates to 1704 (the second floor was built in 1808). A splendid collection of period antiques culled from a number of old Trinitario families convincingly evokes the life of a local sugar baron in the 1800s. ⏱ *45 min. C/ Fernando H. Echerri 52 esq C/ Simón Bolívar.* ☎ *41/99-4363. Admission CUC$2. Tues–Sat 9am–5pm, last two Suns of month 9am–1pm.*

Plaza Mayor.

❸ **Museo de Arquitectura Colonial.** Located on the east side of the Plaza Mayor, in a sky-blue mansion once belonging to the Sánchez Iznaga family, this museum features moderately interesting exhibits that trace the development of Trinidad, including examples of woodwork and ironwork, maps, models, and photographs. ⏱ *30 min.* ☎ *41/99-3208. Admission CUC$1. Sat–Thurs 9am– 5pm, first two Suns of month 9am–1pm.*

Museo Romántico.

4 La Canchánchara. An open-air courtyard bar in an atmospheric colonial house. Kick back in old wooden chairs and enjoy the eponymous house drink, made with aguardiente (firewater), lime, and honey. *C/ Rubén Martínez Villena esq Pablo P. Girón. No phone. $.*

Museo de la Lucha Contra Bandidos.

5 ★ Museo Histórico Municipal. The former Palacio Cantero, an 1830 palatial residence built by a noted sugar baron, now houses a museum. In addition to antiques and 19th-century furnishings, there are exhibits on slave history, revolutionary Cuba, and old bank notes. For many visitors, though, the highlight is the climb up the narrow and rickety wooden stairs to the tower, which has terrific bird's-eye views over Trinidad and its surrounds. ⏱ *1 hr. Simón Bolívar 423 e/ Peña and Gustavo Izquierdo* ☎ *41/99-4460. Admission CUC$2. Sat–Thurs 9am–5pm.*

6 Museo de la Lucha Contra Bandidos. The second of Trinidad's two major towers is the picturesque, green-and-cream domed bell tower belonging to the former 18th-century **Convento de San Francisco** (Convent of Saint Francis of Assisi). Today the building hosts this dogmatic but fascinating museum that focuses on revolutionary Cuba and the continuing 'struggle against bandits.' Exhibits document Fidel's battles against counter-revolutionaries—the *bandidos* in question—who sought to overthrow the regime's ideals by winning support among *guajiros* (poor rural farmers) and fighting in the Sierra del Escambray in the 1960s. In addition to newspaper reports, you'll find machine guns, military maps, a CIA radio, and photos of the ragtag principals who finally, and quite extraordinarily, overthrew the Batista government in 1959. The biggest draw, however, may be the panoramic views from the bell tower.

🕐 45 min. C/ Fernando H. Echerri esq Piro Guinart. ☎ 41/99-4121. Admission CUC$1. Tues–Sat 9am–5pm, last two Suns of the month 9am–1pm.

❼ ★★ Valle de los Ingenios.
The Valley of the Sugar Mills was once one of the most productive sugar-cane growing areas in all of Cuba. The gorgeous, verdant valley is no longer king of the sugar trade, which once supported 60 mills, but for visitors, it makes a wonderful day trip. A 1907 American steam

train departs daily for the valley, making the journey out to one of the old sugar estates, Manaca-Iznaga, in just over 30 minutes. The old manor house (Casa Hacienda) remains and is now a tourist restaurant; however, the main attraction is the fantastic, 45m-high (148-foot) pointed tower, built in 1845, which visitors can ascend for a fee (CUC$1) for spectacular views of the surrounding area. The train station is 1km (0.6 mile) from the center of Trinidad on Calle Antonio Guiteras Final. ☎ 41/99-3348. CUC$10 round-trip. Daily departures at 9am, returning 1.30pm.

❽ ★ Playa Ancón. Playa Ancón is a beach with the distinct advantage of being close to Trinidad, just 13km (8 miles) from town. *See p 55.*

❾ ★★ Parque Nacional Topes de Collantes (Sierra del Escambray). Northwest of Trinidad is the pine-covered Sierra del Escambray and the Topes de Collantes National Park. *See p 62.*

The Sweetness of Sugar

Founded in 1514 on the site of a native Taíno settlement, Villa de la Santísima Trinidad was the fourth of Diego Velázquez's original seven *villas* (towns). Trinidad quickly grew and prospered in princely fashion from the sugar-cane industry of the Valle de los Ingenios. The boom that took root in the mid-1700s created a coterie of wealthy local sugar barons, who built magnificent estates in the valley and manor houses in town, and imported thousands of African slaves to work the fields. Trinidad's golden age, however, proved to be short-lived. Slave uprisings on plantations, intense European competition, and finally independence struggles across the Caribbean took their toll on the Cuban sugar industry.

When the bottom dropped out of sugar by the 1860s, Trinidad's economy collapsed. The town drifted into obscurity, escaping the further economic development that would have obscured the colonial nucleus honored by UNESCO as a World Heritage Site in 1988.

Where to **Stay & Dine**

★ **Brisas Trinidad del Mar**
The fanciest beach hotel on Playa Ancón, this place is semi-luxurious and easygoing. The all-inclusive hotel imitates the famed colonial architecture of Trinidad and sits on the best stretch of beach. Rooms are handsomely outfitted. ☎ *41/99-6500. www.hotelescubanacan.com. 241 rooms. CUC$128–197 double all-inclusive. MC, V.*

★★ **Casa Font** A gorgeous, late-18th-century colonial home, this family home has a great collection of antiques: chandeliers of Baccarat crystal, thick wood doors, colonial- and republican-era oil paintings, and fan-shaped windows above doors. Out back is a pretty courtyard. One room has a bed dating from 1800, richly decorated with mother-of-pearl, and a lovely tiled bathroom. *C/ Gustavo Izquierdo 105 e/ Piro Guinart and Simón Bolívar. ☎ 41/99-3683. Two rooms. CUC$25 double. No credit cards.*

Grand Hotel Iberostar Trinidad.

★ **Casa Meyer** A spectacular, 200-year-old colonial home, with a garden courtyard. One bedroom is huge, with antique beds, one decorated with mother-of-pearl, while the other, set back in the garden, boasts a huge, bronze four-poster bed. *C/ Gustavo Izquierdo 111 e/ Piro Guinart and Simón Bolívar. ☎ 41/99-3444. Two rooms. CUC$20–25 double. No credit cards.*

★ **Grand Hotel Iberostar Trinidad** Facing the quiet Parque Céspedes, this restored and remodeled old building is now a refined hotel in the heart of colonial Trinidad. All the rooms are spacious and tastefully done. The best rooms are the second-floor standard ones, nos. 106 through 111, with balconies facing the park. *C/ José Martí and Calle Lino Perez. ☎ 41/99-6073. www.iberostar.com. 40 rooms. CUC$182–450 double w/breakfast. MC, V. Children under 15 not allowed.*

★ **Hostal Casa Muñoz** This charming place, run by Julio and Rosa, is a breezy and centrally located colonial house built in 1800 with a shady patio, plus a rooftop terrace with fantastic views. Julio is a photographer and has considerable advice on Trinidad's cultural scene. *C/ José Martí 401 esq C/ Santiago Escobar. ☎ 41/99-3673. www.casa.trinidadphoto.com. Two rooms. CUC$30–35 double. No credit cards.*

Hostal La Rioja Teresa gives one of the best welcomes in Cuba. Her two en suite rooms are focused around a small garden with a covered terrace; there's also a new rooftop bar. *C/ Frank País 389 e/ C/ Simón Bolívar and C/ Francisco Javier Zerquera. ☎ 41/99-4589. tereleria@yahoo.com.mx. Two rooms. CUC$25 double. No credit cards.*

Trinidad's Nightlife

One of the best spots to hear music is on the steps leading to the **Casa de la Música,** Calle Francisco Javier Zerquera s/n (☎ 41/993414). The **Palenque de los Congos Reales,** C/ Fernando H. Echerri, has an open-air stage where you can sometimes catch a Grupo Folklórico performing Afro-Cuban music and dance. These are events not to be missed. The **Casa de la Trova,** C/ Fernando H. Echerri 29, a block east of the Plaza Mayor, is the traditional spot to listen to Cuban bands. The **Ruinas del Teatro Brunet,** C/ Maceo e/ Zerquera y Simón Bolívar, puts on a nightly Afro-Cuban cabaret-style show in the spacious courtyard of the ruins of the city's first theater. Another bar set in a delightful open-air courtyard in the ostensible ruins of a colonial home, the **Ruinas de Segarte,** C/ Jesús Menéndez s/n, is an intimate affair.

★ **Hotel Las Cuevas** Perched on a hill 1.6km (1 mile) north of (and above) the old colonial core, this hotel is named for the caves that dot the hillside. The 1950s hotel features rows of concrete bungalow-style remodeled rooms and a pool. Finca Santa Ana. ☎ 41/99-6133. *www.hotelescubanacan.com.* 109 *rooms. CUC$70–77 double w/breakfast. MC, V.*

★★ **Paladar Estela** *CRIOLLA* A handful of tables are set in an exuberant colonial garden setting. Portions are nearly as voluminous as the flora. Dishes include roast pork a la cubana, fried chicken, and grilled fish. However, my favorite is the perfectly spiced ropa vieja made with shredded lamb. *C/ Simón Bolívar 557.* ☎ *41/99-4329. Mains CUC$8–10. No credit cards. Mon–Fri 6.30–9pm.*

★★ **Sol y Son** *CRIOLLA* One of Trinidad's long-standing paladares, this place is housed in an art- and furniture-bedecked, 19th-century house. Out back, on the porch of a verdant courtyard, the restaurant offers spaghetti, fish, chicken, and pork dishes. Check out the *cerdo borracho* (drunk pork), which is grilled and doused with rum, and the house cocktail made from seven-year-old rum and honey. *C/ Simón Bolívar 283 e/ C/ José Martí and C/ Frank País. Mains CUC$6–9. No credit cards. Mon–Thurs noon–3pm, Fri–Sun noon–3pm, 6.30–11pm.*

Hostal Casa Muñoz.

Viñales

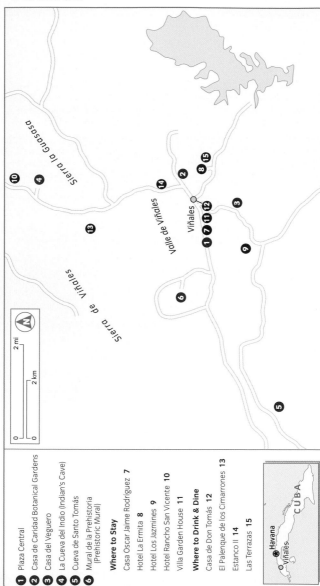

Sierra la Guasasa

Valle de Viñales

Viñales

Sierra de Viñales

0   2 km
0   2 mi

1   Plaza Central
2   Casa de Caridad Botanical Gardens
3   Casa del Veguero
4   La Cueva del Indio (Indian's Cave)
5   Cueva de Santo Tomás
6   Mural de la Prehistoria
     (Prehistoric Mural)

Where to Stay

Casa Oscar Jaime Rodríguez   7
Hotel La Ermita   8
Hotel Los Jazmines   9
Hotel Rancho San Vicente   10
Villa Garden House   11

Where to Drink & Dine

Casa de Don Tomás   12
El Palenque de los Cimarrones   13
Estanco II   14
Las Terrazas   15

CUBA

Havana

Viñales

Viñales is a picturesque town in the heart of Cuba's prime tobacco-growing region. The town itself sits in the center of a flat valley, a UNESCO World Heritage Site, surrounded by karst hill formations known locally as *mogotes*, irregular, steep-sided geological formations that rise as high as 300m (1000 feet) and have bases ranging from just a few hundred meters in diameter to as much as a couple of kilometers in length. The Viñales Valley is a great spot to bicycle around, and there are good options for bird-watching, hiking, horse-riding, and in particular rock climbing and spelunking. The view of the Valley from any of the surrounding hillsides is stunning, particularly at sunrise or sunset.

❶ Plaza Central. The center of the village focuses around the small plaza with its charming white church with a green dome. In the corner of the Plaza is the popular music venue **Patio de Polo Montañez,** named after one of Cuba's most famous singers who died an untimely death in a car accident in 2002.

❷ ★ Casa de Caridad Botanical Gardens. One of the nicer attractions in Viñales is this spot at the northeastern end of town. The lush gardens feature a mix of ornamental and medicinal plants and flowers, as well as orchids, bromeliads, palms, and fruit trees. If you're really lucky, you'll be able to munch on freshly harvested fruit. ⏱ *15 min-1 hr. Donations warmly accepted. Daily 9am–6pm.*

❸ Casa del Veguero. The Viñales Valley is part of the heart of Cuba's tobacco-growing region and a great place to take a tobacco tour. Typical tours start at this *bohío*, a small farm that grows and dries the primary material, followed by a visit to the nearby de-veining station, or *despalilladora*. Here, you'll see workers handle and sort the prized leaves for the *capas* (outer layers). You might also be given a quick tour of a final curing station, where the

Ploughing oxen, Viñales Valley.

Casa de Caridad Botanical Gardens.

leaves emit an ammonia gas that makes your eyes water. Finally, you'll visit a local cigar shop. ⏲ *1 hr. Carretera a Hotel los Jazmines.* ☎ *48/79-6080. Free admission. Daily 9.30am–5.30pm.*

4 La Cueva del Indio (Indian's Cave). Caves abound in Viñales, and are among its major attractions. This cave is the most popular, and gets its name from the fact that indigenous remains were found here. Only 1km (0.6 mile) or so of the extensive system is open to tourists. A well-lit path leads from the entrance through a few small and narrow galleries to a tiny dock on an underground river. This is the easiest of the cave trips in the area. Here, you board a small rowboat powered by an outboard engine for a quick trip of about 180m (600 feet) up and down this river, before exiting the cave at a dock area. ⏲ *45 min. 5km (3 miles) north of Viñales*

at Km 33, Carretera de Puerto Esperanza. ☎ *48/79-6280. Admission CUC\$5. Daily 9am–5pm.*

5 ★ Cueva de Santo Tomás. Those with an interest in more serious spelunking should head to these caves. With over 45km (28 miles) of connected tunnels, chambers, and galleries, it's the largest explored cave system in Cuba. Some of the chambers and galleries are quite massive, with impressive stalagmite and stalactite formations. Unlike La Cueva del Indio, this cave system has been left in its natural state and you must carry headlamps and flashlights. So far, a relatively simple 1km (0.6 mile) section has been opened for guided tours, although more adventurous spelunking tours are in the works. ⏲ *1–1½ hrs. Visits including guide and equipment cost CUC\$10. Tours can be booked in advance with the Centro de Visitantes, located on the highway into Viñales, just beyond the Hotel Los Jazmines, or at the site. No phone. Daily 9.30am–4pm; last departure 3pm. See also p 22.*

6 Mural de la Prehistoria (Prehistoric Mural). Despite being big, this over-hyped attraction is decidedly uninteresting as art, woefully inadequate as narrative, and just not impressive enough in execution to merit all the attention it gets. And it can't quite cut it as kitsch. Despite some fresh paint, which restored—and even improved on—the vibrant colors of artist Leovigildo González Morillo's original work, this massive mural lacks the style and weight of the works of Morillo's mentor, Diego Rivera. ⏲ *10 secs. 4km (2½ miles) west of Viñales.* ☎ *48/79-6260. Admission CUC\$1 (waived if you eat at the on-site restaurant). Daily 8am–7pm.*

Where to **Stay**

Casa Oscar Jaime Rodríguez
This is a large family home with the rooms spread around a central courtyard festooned with plants and flowers and featuring rocking chairs and a pizza oven. The choice room is the one upstairs with its own balcony. There's a communal dining area. The friendly family is helpful with local information. *C/ Adela Azcuy 43.* ☎ *48/79-3381. ljaime@uci.cu. Two rooms CUC$20 double. No credit cards.*

Hotel La Ermita
Similar in style and setting to Hotel Los Jazmines (see below), this modest hotel is set on the hillside just above Viñales. There are excellent views from the grounds and restaurant, although only 12 rooms have the area's signature vista. Rooms in the newer buildings have a private porch or balcony with Adirondack chairs. The poolside barbecue restaurant is preferable to the hotel's buffet option. *Carretera de La Ermita Km 1.5, Viñales.* ☎ *48/79-6071. www.hotelescubanacan.com. 62 rooms. CUC$79–87 double w/breakfast. MC, V.*

★ Hotel Los Jazmines
Most of the rooms in this attractive hotel are housed in two three-story buildings set on a hillside overlooking the Viñales Valley. Touches of gingerbread wrought-iron work and stained glass give the place elegance. If possible, request a top-floor room in the newer block, nos. 301 to 316. *Carretera de Viñales Km 25.* ☎ *48/79-6205. www.hoteles cubanacan.com. 78 rooms. CUC$70– 120 double w/breakfast. MC, V.*

★ Hotel Rancho San Vicente
Located north of the Cueva del Indio, this quiet nature hotel can almost be considered a spa. A half-dozen or so semi-private soaking pools (CUC$5) are fed by tepid mineral springs, and massage and mud treatments are available (CUC$15). Most of the rooms are individual little bungalows. By far the best are the 20 new units housed in a series of two-story wooden buildings spread around the grounds, amid a shady grove of pine, palm, and fruit trees. *Carretera de Puerto Esperanza Km 33.* ☎ *48/79-6201. www.hotelescubanacan.com. 53 rooms. CUC$70–82 double w/ breakfast. MC, V.*

Villa Garden House.
Located on the main street, this elegant old house, run by Dulce María Junco and Bienvenido Nuñez, has one

Hotel Los Jazmines.

Viñales Nightlife

Viñales has a couple of low-key bars on its main street. If you're lucky, there might be a concert at the local **Casa de la Cultura,** or the hugely popular **Patio de Polo Montáñez** (see ❶), or at the nearby smaller ARTex venue, **Patio del Decimista. Discoteca Las Cuevas** is located at the entrance to El Palenque de los Cimarrones. Flashing lights and loud music get an atmospheric boost from the hanging stalactites. There's a cabaret show here on Saturdays at 9pm; admission is CUC$3.

room equipped with a double and single bed. Relax on the back porch surrounded by a garden of flowers and vegetables. *C/ Salvador Cisneros 44.* ☎ *48/79-3297. One room. CUC$15–20. No credit cards.*

Where to **Drink & Dine**

Casa de Don Tomás *CRIOLLA/ SPANISH* This famous state restaurant, set in a blue 1889 colonial mansion, was semi-destroyed by 2008's hurricanes and had a temporary home opposite the original site in mid-2009. Signature dish, *Las Delicias de Don Tomás*, is a paella-like dish of Spanish rice cooked and served in an earthenware bowl with chicken, pork, fish, ham, and even lobster. *Opposite C/ Salvador Cisnero 140.* ☎ *48/79-6300. Mains CUC$5–14. No credit cards. Daily 10am–10pm.*

★ El Palenque de los Cimarrones *CRIOLLA* Although this is definitely a tourist trap, the food is surprisingly good, and the show and setting are informative without being too kitsch. At the end of the restaurant's entrance path is a re-creation of one of the homes set up by runaway slaves who lived and hid in the caves. After some brief Afro-Cuban music and dance, you reach the restaurant, which is a series of interconnected thatched huts, each representing a different *orisha* (Afro-Cuban deity).

The main dish is a slow-roasted chicken seasoned with oregano, cumin, garlic, and lime juice—it's excellent. *Km 36 on highway to Puerto Esperanza, north of Viñales.* ☎ *48/79-6290. Mains CUC$5–5.80. No credit cards. Daily 11am–4pm.*

Estanco II *ITALIAN* An attractive roadside *ranchón* (café) popular with Cubans and foreigners. Close to the botanic garden, it serves up reasonable, good-value pizzas with efficient service. Opt for the *pizza especial* because it's tastier and leaves you fuller. *Road to La Cueva del Indio, Viñales. No phone. Mains CUC$3–8. No credit cards. Daily 10am–10pm.*

Las Terrazas *CRIOLLA* This hotel restaurant has a wonderful view over the Viñales Valley. Standard Cuban cuisine features, but there are a few twists: for example, turkey fricassee, a turkey meat stewed in a tomato and white-wine sauce. Arrive in time for the sunset. *Hotel La Ermita, Carretera de La Ermita. Km 1.5.* ☎ *48/ 79-6071. Mains CUC$4.85–9.85. MC, V. Daily 7am–10pm.* ●

The
Savvy Traveler

Before You Go

Government Tourist Offices

In the US: Cuban Interests Section, 2630 16th St, NW, Washington DC, 20009, ☎ 202/797-8518, http:// embacu.cubaminrex.cu.

In Canada: Cuba Tourist Board Canada 1200 Bay St., Suite 305, Toronto ON M5R 2A5, ☎ 416/362-0700, www.gocuba.ca.

Cuba Tourist Board Canada, 2075 rue Université, Bureau 460, Montreal, Quebec H3A 2L1, ☎ 514/848-0668.

In the UK: Cuba Tourist Board Great Britain, 154 Shaftesbury Ave., 1st Floor, London, WC2H 8HL, ☎ 0207/240-6655, tourism@cubasi.info.

Useful Websites

The official tourism websites for Cuba are **www.cubatravel.cu, www.cubasi.cu,** and **www. dtcuba.com.** State-run tourism agency websites—including Cubanacán **(www.cubanacan.cu)** and Cubatur **(www.cubatur.cu)**— are also good places to check for hotels, transportation, and package deals. Infotur **(www.infotur.cu),** based in Cuba, also provides fairly detailed information on the country's provinces through a series of downloadable PDFs. The Latin America Network Information Center **(http://lanic.utexas.edu/la/cb/cuba)** is hands down the best one-stop shop for helpful links to a wide range of travel and general information sites.

To read travelogs about Cuba, try the forum section at **www.cuba mania.com. http://havanajournal. com** is another site that collates a huge amount of up-to-date news, culture, and tourism stories.

Visa Information

Although it's not illegal for US citizens to travel to Cuba, most are prohibited from spending any money in Cuba. This, in effect, is the 'travel ban.' The complicated prohibition, which allows for various exceptions, is governed by the US Treasury Department and the Office of Foreign Assets Control (OFAC). Further information can be found at www.treas. gov/offices/enforcement/ofac/ programs/cuba/cuba.shtml. Here you can find out about licensed travel to Cuba using authorized Travel Service Providers; see p 162.

Many Americans travel to Cuba as unlicensed travelers through third countries such as Mexico and Canada. Although this is against the law in the US, you will encounter no problems at immigration in Cuba; however, Cuban immigration have been known to stamp US passports of unlicensed travelers.

Tourist visas cost CUC$22–35, depending upon the issuing agent, and are good for up to 90 days for US and Canadian citizens, although customs agents will sometimes issue them for just 30 days, or until the date of your return flight, unless you request otherwise. This is especially the case for unlicensed US travelers. The visas can be extended for another 30 days once you arrive in Cuba for an additional minimum CUC$25 although it has been known for US citizens to be granted a total of six months. In order to extend your tourist visa, you must go to any immigration office in the country. An additional 90-day extension for Canadians can be granted once for a cost of approximately CUC$22. For further information, contact the Cuban Embassy at www.embacubacanada. net; or the Cuban consulate in Toronto at cubacon1@on.aibn.com; or see the Cuba tourist board in Canada website at www.gocuba.ca.

Cuban Americans with close relatives in Cuba may now visit as often as they wish with no time restriction on the visit, but they remain limited to daily expenditure rates of US$179 in the country.

In the UK, if you buy a ticket for an independent flight, you will need to purchase a separate tourist visa. The visa is available from the Cuban Embassy in London for £15 plus postage (www.cubaldn.com), but the cheapest and most efficient place to buy one is directly from www.visacuba.co.uk. UK citizens are granted entry for 30 days. This can be extended once only at any immigration office for an additional 30 days for CUC$25. Note that when seeking a tourist visa extension, you need to purchase bank stamps for the value of the extension you need. Ask your hotel or casa owner for advice.

The Best Time To Go

The tourist high season runs from December through March, coinciding with the winter months in most northern countries. It also coincides with Cuba's dry season. Throughout this season, and especially around the Christmas and Easter holidays, the beaches and resorts are relatively full, prices are somewhat higher, and it may be harder to find an available rental car or room. In addition, overbooking—a widespread problem in the Cuban tourism industry—is certainly much more of a problem during the high season. During the low season, you should be able to find discounts on rooms, car rentals, and tour options. Moreover, resorts and attractions are much less crowded. However, temperatures are somewhat higher throughout the low season and periods of extended rainfall are not uncommon.

Public Holidays

Cuba has a very limited number of official holidays, and aside from Christmas Day, no religious holidays are recognized by the state. Official holidays are: January 1 (Liberation Day), May 1 (Labor Day), July 26 (Revolution Day), October 10 (anniversary of the beginning of the 1868 War of Independence), and December 25 (Christmas Day). Other important dates that sometimes bring Cuba to a de facto state of national holiday include: January 28 (Birth of José Marti), February 24 (anniversary of the beginning of the 1895 War of Independence), March 8 (International Women's Day), April 19 (anniversary of Bay of Pigs victory), July 30 (Day of the Martyrs of the Revolution), October 8 (anniversary of the death of Che Guevara), October 28 (anniversary of the death of Camilo Cienfuegos), and December 7 (anniversary of the death of Antonio Maceo).

Other Festivals & Events

SPRING The mid-February Havana **International Jazz Festival** usually draws a handful of top international bands and soloists to share the stage and billing with a strong stable of Cuba's best jazz talents. (www.festivaljazzplaza.icm.cu).

Run by the official state cigar company, Habanos, S.A., the **Habanos Festival** includes lectures, factory visits, tastings, and a gala dinner with an auction of rare cigars in Havana in late February. (www.habanos.com).

The **Havana Biennale** is one of the premier Latin American art shows, occurring in odd numbered years in April. (www.bienalhabana.cult.cu).

SUMMER Theaters, clubs, and concert halls across Havana are filled with the sweet and melancholy sounds of bolero in late June for the **International Festival 'Boleros de Oro'.**

The **Fiesta del Fuego** features concerts, parades, and street fairs that celebrate Afro-Caribbean culture in Santiago de Cuba from July 3–9. (www.casadelcaribe.cult.cu).

Santiago de Cuba, the most 'African' city in Cuba, throws an excellent annual **Carnival** in the days before and after July 26.

FALL Cuba's national saint, the Virgin of Cobre, is revered by Roman Catholics and Santeros alike at the **Fiesta de la Virgen del Cobre**. There are pilgrimages to her altar in the small town of El Cobre on September 8.

The silky sounds of the **International Festival 'Matamoros Son'** fill the streets and theaters of Santiago in mid-October.

The Cuban National Ballet, still one of the most highly regarded troupes on the planet, stages the wonderful annual **Havana International Ballet Festival** in the Gran Teatro de La Habana in late October. (www.balletcuba.cult.cu).

WINTER The **International Festival of New Latin American Film** is one of the premier film festivals in Latin America. A packed schedule of films is shown in movie theaters over a period of 10 days throughout Havana in early December. (www.habanafilmfestival.com).

Las Parrandas, an extravagant public carnival, features late-night parades with ornate floats, costumed revelers, and a serious amount of fireworks. The big event occurs on 24 December in Remedios.

If no specific contact information for a particular event is offered, contact **Paradiso** (☎ 7/836-4931; www.paradiso.cu/eventos.asp), the tour agency arm of the national arts and cultural organization ARTex. You

can also find pretty reliable festival information at www.cubatravel.cu and www.cult.cu (in Spanish only).

The Weather
Cuba has two distinct seasons, rainy (May–Oct) and dry (Nov–Apr). The dry season is characterized by consistently sunny and temperate weather, with daytime temperatures averaging between 24 to 27°C (75–80°F). However, temperature swings are greater during this period, and it can actually get somewhat chilly when cold fronts—or 'northers'—creep down the eastern seaboard of the United States, particularly in January and February. In contrast, the rainy season is overall a slightly warmer period, with less dramatic same-day temperature swings. There's a dry spell most years during August, which is also the hottest month. The annual hurricane season runs June–November, with September and October having the highest number of hurricanes.

Cell Phones
Cell phone coverage is good all over Cuba, but check with your network provider to make sure your phone will work in the country. In Cuba, cellular service is controlled by Cubacel, Av 5 and C/ 76, Edificio Barcelona, Centro de Negocios, Miramar (☎ 5/264-2266; www.cubacel.cu). Cubacel offers cell phones for rental at CUC$6 per day with a CUC$3 daily activation fee. Cubacel works with both TMA and GSM systems.

Pre-paid calling cards are sold widely. Using a Cubacel account it costs CUC$0.50–0.60 to make a call to a land line, depending on the time of day, and CUC$0.36–0.44 to receive one. Between cell phones it costs CUC$0.44–0.50 to call and CUC$0.36–0.40 to receive. It costs CUC$0.16 to SMS and CUC$1 for

AVERAGE TEMPERATURE & RAINFALL IN CUBA

MONTH	HOURS OF SUNSHINE	RAIN (IN MM)	MAXIMUM TEMPERATURE (IN °C)	MINIMUM TEMPERATURE (IN °C)	SEA TEMPERATURE (IN °C)
January	6	71	26	18	25
February	6	46	26	18	25
March	7	46	27	19	25
April	7	58	29	21	26
May	8	119	30	22	28
June	6	165	31	23	29
July	6	125	32	24	30
August	6	135	32	24	31
September	5	150	31	24	30
October	5	173	29	23	29
November	5	79	27	21	28
December	5	58	26	19	27

one SMS to an international number. International visitors who take their phone to Cuba should check whether their service provider has an agreement with Cubacel and if so what the (inevitably expensive) rates will be. North American phones do not work in Cuba because there is no roaming agreement between US cell service providers and Cuba. However, this situation may change.

Car Rentals
It could work out cheaper, and it will certainly remove the hassle, if you book your car hire at home. In the UK, try CubaDirect (www.cubadirect. co.uk). In Cuba, Via Rent a Car (☎ 7/861-4465. www.gaviota-grupo.com. Licensed US Travel Service Providers (see p 162) can arrange this for you.

Getting **There**

By Plane
José Martí International Airport (☎ 7/266-4133) is 18km (11 miles) southwest of central Havana. Varadero International Airport is 23km (14 miles) from the center of Varadero. The national airline, Cubana (☎ 7/834-4446; www.cubana.cu), operates flights between Cuba and Toronto, Europe, the Caribbean, and other Latin American cities. Aerocaribbean (☎ 7/879-7524; www.aerocaribbean.com) also flies to Cuba

from the Caribbean and Central America.

From the UK: Flying time is 10 hours from London. Virgin Atlantic (☎ 0870-380-2007; www.virgin-atlantic.com) runs twice-weekly services all year from London Gatwick. Cubana (☎ 0207-538-5933) operates twice-weekly regular services from London Gatwick to Havana with a stop in Holguín on the inbound service. Thomas Cook (☎ 0871/895-0055) flies from Gatwick and Manchester to Cayo Coco,

Holguín, and Varadero. During summer months it also flies from Manchester to Cayo Santa María and from Glasgow to Cayo Coco. Thomson (☎ 0871/231-4691) flies to Varadero and Holguín.

From Europe: Cuba is served by flights from Spain with Iberia (☎ 0870/380-2007 in the UK) and Air Europa (☎ 0207/153-6925 in the UK); from France with Air France (☎ 0870/142-4343 in the UK); and from the Netherlands with Martinair (☎ 31/20-601-1767 in the Netherlands).

From Canada: Air Canada (☎ 888/247-2262) and Cubana (☎ 888/667-1222) run scheduled flights. Charter flights also operate.

From elsewhere in the world: Cuba is served by flights from Mexico, Jamaica, the Dominican Republic, Grand Cayman, and the Bahamas.

From the US: There is no regular scheduled service between the United States and Cuba, although numerous charter flights leave from Miami, and to a lesser extent from New York and Los Angeles. Licensed US travelers are eligible to use these flights. Unlicensed travelers must pass through a third country such as Mexico or Canada.

Check the following airline websites for full details on schedules and services: Aeroméxico (www. aeromexico.com); Air Canada (www.aircanada.com); Air France (www.airfrance.com); Air Jamaica (www.airjamaica.com); Air Transat (www.airtransat.com); Alitalia (www.alitalia.com); Aviacsa (www. aviacsa.com.mx); Bahamasair (www. bahamasair.com); Cayman Airways (www.caymanairways.com); Grupo Taca (www.taca.com); Iberia Airlines (www.iberia.com); Martinair (www. martinair.com); Mexicana (www. mexicana.com); Air Comet (www. aircomet.com); Air Europa (www. aireuropa.com); Blue Panorama (www.blue-panorama.com); Condor

Airways (www3.condor.com); Thomas Cook (www.thomascook. com); Thomson (www.thomson. co.uk).

By Package Tour

Many visitors to Cuba travel via an organized tour, which includes a package of flights and accommodation. This is often the cheapest way to travel to Cuba and there are plenty of companies offering these deals. Below are a handful of UK, Canadian, and licensed US travel agencies offering packages. Also check prices via online travel agencies, because it's possible to grab a bargain online.

CANADA:

Signature Travel, www.signature vacations.com.
Air Transat Holidays, www.airtrans atholidays.com.

USA:

ABC Charters, www.abc-charters. com.
Tico Travel, www.destinationcuba. com.

UK:

Cuba Direct, www.cubadirect.co.uk.
Cubaism, www.cubaism.com.
Regent Holidays, www.south americanexperience.co.uk.
Travel Republic, www.travel republic.co.uk.
Thomas Cook, www.thomascook.com.

By Special Interest Tour
GENERAL

GAP Adventures (☎ 800/708-7761 in the US and Canada, or 0870/999-0144 in the UK; www.gapadventures. com).

Global Exchange (☎ 800/497-1994, ext 242; www.globalexchange. org).

ADVENTURE & WELLNESS TRIPS

Most tour operators listed can arrange trekking tours. Caledonia (☎ 0131/621-7721; www.caledonia languages.com) organizes trekking trips in the Sierra Maestra. There is

Money Saving Tips

If you aren't traveling via a package tour, book accommodation in advance of your visit via Internet travel sites or directly online with the hotel or resort where you plan to stay. It's often possible to save a fortune. For more information on accommodation in Cuba, check www.cubahotelreservations.com, www.cubaism.com, www.casaparticular.info, www.casaparticular.org, and www.cubacasas.net. Travel is cheaper in low season. In Cuba that falls between April (post-Easter) and June, and between September and October. In addition, carry as much cash to Cuba as you can; bank card fees (see p 167) are extortionate.

only one fully oriented spa center independent of hotels in Cuba, the Acuavida Centro Spa-Taloso on Cayo Coco. Cuba Direct (☎ 0844/415-5510; www.cubadirect.co.uk) can organize week-long trips including flights, transfers, and four days of treatments.

BIRDWATCHING
Cuba Welcome (☎ 020/7731-6871 in the UK; www.cubawelcome.com). Canadian Operation Quest Nature Tours (☎ 416/633-5666; www.questnaturetours.com). See also Chapter 4 The Great Outdoors, p 49.

CIGARS
Cuba Welcome (☎ 020/7731-6871 in the UK; www.cubawelcome.com) offers a five-day cigar tour.
Cycling
Wow Cuba (☎ 800/969-2822 or 902/368-2453; www.wowcuba.com).

DIVING
Specialist operators include Avalon (www.divingincuba.com) and Scuba en Cuba (☎ 01895/624100 in the UK; www.scuba-en-cuba.com).

FISHING
There's a broad network of state-run marinas all around Cuba; the greatest number are run by Grupo Empresarial de Náutica y Marinas Marlin (www.nauticamarlin.com)

and Gaviota (☎ 7/66-9668; www.gaviota-grupo.com). All offer sport-fishing charters. Cuba Welcome (www.cubawelcome.com) and Avalon (www.avalonfishingcenter.com) run reputable operations.

LANGUAGE & CULTURE
The University of Havana (www.uh.cu/infogral/estudiaruh/postgrado/english.html) offers language and culture classes. The University of the Oriente in Santiago de Cuba also offers Spanish classes. On its website (www.uo.edu.cu), click on 'Estudios'. Caledonia (☎ 0131/621-7721; www.caledonialanguages.com) offers Spanish courses in Havana and Santiago.

MOUNTAIN & ROCK CLIMBING
Excellent opportunities abound, especially around the Viñales Valley. Cuba Climbing (www.cubaclimbing.com) can point you to the right rocks.

MUSIC & DANCE TRIPS
Caledonia (☎ 0131/621-7721; www.caledonialanguages.com) offers music and dance trips to Cuba; it's possible to combine these activities with language classes. The site has links to the annual Cuban Music School (www.jazzsummerschool.com/cuban_music_school).

PHOTOGRAPHY TRIPS
Cuba Welcome (☎ 020/7731-6871 in the UK; www.cubawelcome.com) arranges photography workshop tours with British photographer Keith Cardwell. Tours are run in conjunction with Cuban photographer Julio Muñoz, based in Trinidad (www.trinidadphoto.com).

VOLUNTEER & WORKING TRIPS
The Cuban Solidarity Campaign (☎ 020/8800-0155; www.cuba-solidarity.org/brigades.asp) runs international work brigades twice a year for up to 22 days. See also Global Exchange, p. 162.

Getting **Around**

Cuba is approximately 1300km (810 miles) long and traveling around can take significant amounts of time, not only due to the distances but because of the state of some of the roads and the ubiquitous lack of signage. There's a good tourist bus service across the island linking the country's most touristy centers. Car hire from a variety of agencies is available across the country and gas stations are plentiful. This is a flexible, although not cheap, way to see the country.

Street addresses in the text are abbreviated. Calle is shortened to C/ and entre (between) to e/. Esquina (corner) is shortened to esq. The letter y means and. S/n means sin número (an address without a street number).

By Bus

Víazul (☎ 7/881-1413; www.viazul. com) buses are modern and comfortable with lavatories on board. Since the tickets must be paid in hard currency, which precludes many Cubans from using them, there is less demand and greater availability. The main Víazul station is located in Nuevo Vedado, Havana, across from the metropolitan zoo. You can also book Víazul tickets in the international airport and at Infotur (C/ Obispo esq Bernaza. ☎ 7/866-333; www.infotur. cu) in La Habana Vieja. The most expensive fare is CUC$55.08 from Havana to Santiago.

By Car

Driving a rental car is an excellent way to travel around Cuba. Many roads are in acceptable condition, though plenty are severely substandard. And, although there's very little traffic, you have to keep a sharp eye out for horse-drawn carriages, slow-moving tractors, scores of cyclists, and pedestrians taking over major roadways.

There are several state-run car-rental companies, with a large, modern fleet of rental cars to choose from. These include Cubacar (☎ 7/273-2277 cubacar@transtur. cu), Havanautos (☎ 7/835-3142 havanautos@transtur.cu), Rex (☎ 7/835-6830), Transtur (☎ 7/862-2686, www.transtur.cu), and Vía Rent a Car (☎ 7/861-4465 www. gaviota-grupo.com).

Prices and selection are rather standard, with an abundance of small, economy Japanese and Korean cars. A rental car should cost you CUC$45–80 per day, including daily insurance of CUC$10–15 and unlimited mileage, depending on the model and the season. Discounts are available for multiday rentals. Your national driving license is required to rent a car.

It's always a good idea to make a reservation in advance, especially during peak periods, when cars can get a little scarce. However, there's a catch-22 here, in that many of the state-run agencies don't have a trustworthy international reservations system. When demand outstrips supply, the car-rental agencies will often not honor your supposedly confirmed reservation.

It may, therefore, be more reliable to make your reservations through your home country. This is known to be cheaper anyway.

Driving
Driving is generally easy and stress free, but there are a couple of concerns for most foreign drivers here. First (and most annoying) is the fact that there are very, very few road signs and directional aids. Second, there's the issue of hitchhikers. Cuba's public transportation network is grossly overburdened and hitchhiking is a way of life. The highways sometimes seem like one long line, with periodic swellings, of people asking for a lift, or botella. Picking up hitchhikers after dark is to be discouraged. You can, however, stop at an official botella point, identified by the mustard-yellow uniformed official with a clipboard.

It's the law to stop at all rail crossings, and it's also an important safety measure. Cuba's railroad network criss-crosses its highway system at numerous points. Trains rarely slow down and even rarer still are protective crossbars or warning lights.

Drive on the right hand side of the road. At roundabouts vehicles on the left hand side have right of way. The speed limit for cars is 50kph (30 mph) in the cities, 90kph (55 mph) on other roads, and 100kph (62 mph) on the Autopista. It's compulsory for the driver and front seat passenger to wear a seatbelt.

Driving at night isn't advised because there's no lighting on highways. Animal-drawn transport, some trucks, bicycles, and pedestrians are also not illuminated, giving rise to highly dangerous driving situations.

In all cities, there are parqueos (parking lots) where you can leave your vehicle attended for 24 hours. This costs CUC$1–2 a night. It may be unwise to leave the vehicle unattended in cities at night, as theft of wheels and wipers is not unknown.

Breakdown Cover
Your car rental company will provide you with a 24-hour number to call in case of breakdown.

By Taxi
Taxi fares are set by the government. You can catch a taxi at the airport from the rank outside, from Parque Central, the Hotel Nacional, and close to the cathedral in Havana, as well as at most bus stations across the island. Plenty of taxis *particulares* (private cars) also hover. They are not legally allowed to transport foreigners but they will in order to earn hard currency. If they are stopped by the police they will be fined; the foreign passenger is not punished. At some provincial bus stations you will have no other option but to take one.

Airport transfers and taxis can also be booked via your hotel or *casa particular* (private rented room), via Cubataxi ☎ 7/855-5555.

All tourist taxis have meters. Typical fares are: from the airport to La Habana Vieja CUC$20–25, and from La Habana Vieja to Vedado CUC$4–6. Many taxis in Havana attempt to rip-off tourists by not turning on the meter. Be wary. Note that flash, larger modern taxis charge more than the yellow, cheaper-looking vehicles.

Fast **Facts**

ATMS   Every city in Cuba has one or two ATMs. Currency exchange bureaux (CADECAs) can be found all over the island.

BANKING HOURS   Banks are normally open 8am–4pm Monday to Friday. Some open on Saturday mornings.

BUSINESS HOURS   Shops are usually open 9am–5pm Monday to Saturday. In beach resort areas shops may remain open until 9pm.

CELL PHONES   See p 160.

CREDIT CARDS   Visa and MasterCard credit cards of non-US issue are accepted in most hotels. They are not accepted in *casas particulares*.

CUSTOMS   Travelers may export up to 50 cigars with no questions asked. Larger quantities can be exported, provided you show proof that they were bought in official Habanos S.A. outlets. There are restrictions on certain works of art, books, publications, and coins. Travelers are officially limited to taking home two bottles of rum or other spirits, although this limit is rarely enforced. The usual rules apply on importing goods through customs into your home country.

DOCTORS   See 'Hospitals', below.

DRUGSTORES   See 'Pharmacies', below.

ELECTRICITY   110-volt AC, and most outlets are US-style two- or three-prong. However, many of the large hotels and resorts that cater primarily to a Canadian and European clientele are wired for 220 volts.

EMBASSIES & CONSULATES   Canada, C/ 30 no. 518, esq Av 7, Miramar (☎ 7/204-2516; http://havana.gc.ca). **United Kingdom,** C/ 34 no. 704, e/ Av 7 and 17, Miramar (☎ 7/214-2200; www.britishembassy.gov.uk/cuba). **United States** Interests Section, C/ Calzada e/ C/ L and M, Vedado (☎ 7/833-3551; http://havana.usinterestsection.gov) is the official US government representation on the island. **Australia/New Zealand** There is no representation in Cuba. Consular assistance is provided by the embassies in Mexico. Assistance can be given to Australian citizens by the Canadian embassy in Havana.

EMERGENCY ASSISTANCE   Police ☎ 106, **Ambulance** ☎ 104, **Fire Emergency** ☎ 106.

GAY AND LESBIAN TRAVELERS Homosexuality is not illegal in Cuba, but in general the country has a poor record on gay and lesbian rights. Although the situation has improved somewhat in recent years, there are still high levels of homophobia and broad societal rejection of gays and lesbians.

HOLIDAYS   For details of Cuba's national holidays, see p 159.

HOSPITALS   A full list of international clinics, international drugstores, and opticians is available on the **Servimed** website (www.servimedcuba.com//en/directory.php). The **Clinica Central Cira García,** C/ 20 no. 4101, esq Av 41, Playa, Havana (☎ 7/204-2811; www.cirag.cu) is the largest medical center in the country catering to foreigners.

There are also a number of international clinics in main towns throughout the island where you can see a doctor. Check with your hotel or casa for details of the one closest to your accommodation.

INSURANCE   Always travel with adequate insurance cover. If you plan to undertake high-risk activities, such as diving, make sure your policy covers these activities. **Asistur,** Prado 208 e/ C/ Trocadero and

Colón (☎ 7/866-4499; 7/866-8521 emergency number; www.asistur.cu) will help you with medical reports and the management of medical expenses if you end up in the hospital. Its addresses outside Havana are available at www.asistur.cu/mapa.html.

INTERNET ACCESS/CAFÉS Internet is available in all large towns in the Etecsa offices at a rate of CUC$6/hr via a card that's valid for 30 days. Some hotels also have their own terminals; the fee is the same. WiFi is available at only a handful of hotels in Cuba for CUC$8 per hour.

LOST PROPERTY Contact the police in your location. Ask your hotel or casa for advice.

MAIL & POSTAGE Central Havana's main post office is next to the Gran Teatro on Parque Central. Opening hours are 8am–5pm Monday to Saturday.

MONEY & EXCHANGE BUREAUS The Cuban Convertible Peso (CUC) is an internationally unsupported currency and is, for all intents and purposes, pegged to the US dollar. All the CADECA (exchange branches) and major banks will change US dollars, euros, British pounds, and Canadian dollars.

There are, in fact, two distinct kinds of currency circulating: the *moneda libremente convertible* ('convertible peso' or CUC) and the *moneda nacional* (Cuban peso or MN). Both are distinguished by the dollar ($) symbol. Both the CUC and *moneda nacional* are divided into units of 100 centavos.

At the time of writing, the convertible peso official exchange rate is US$1 = CUC$.93 and £1 = CUC$1.37. However, US dollars are penalized by a 10% surcharge on all money exchange operations into convertible pesos. Euros, British pounds, or Canadian dollars are freely exchanged at all CADECA branches

and most banks around Cuba. Cuban banks will sometimes refuse to accept bills with even slight tears or markings. Convertible pesos come in 1, 3, 5, 10, 20, 50, and 100 peso bills. Convertible peso coins come in denominations of 1, 5, 10, 25, and 50 centavos, and 1 centavo.

Currently, Cuban pesos can be exchanged legally for CUC (and vice versa) at any CADECA money exchange office. The official exchange rate as of press time was around 25 Cuban pesos to the CUC. Although opportunities for travelers to pay in Cuban pesos are few and far between, it's not a bad idea to exchange around CUC$1–2 for pesos soon after arrival. It may be possible to pay for some meals, movie tickets, and other goods or services in Cuban pesos, and the savings are substantial. If 'MN' is displayed on the prices, you should theoretically be paying Cuban pesos. However, in most cases, vendors will try to insist that any non-Cuban pay in convertible pesos, often at a one-to-one rate of exchange.

It's best to travel to Cuba with as much cash as you feel comfortable carrying because you're fabulously ripped off when taking money out on your debit or credit card. No matter what the country of origin of your card, your transaction will first be converted into US dollars, thereby incurring a charge of up to 12.5%, before you are given the CUC$. This also happens at ATMs where your request for CUC$ is converted to US dollars at that day's exchange rate. You're then charged a CUC$ commission in US dollars at the point of withdrawal.

NEWSPAPERS, MAGAZINES & TV The state-run Communist daily newspaper Granma is published in English in an international edition on a weekly basis. You can read it online in English too: www.granma.cu/ingles/index.html. The daily version is available on the streets or from kiosks for MN$0.20. It carries TV listings and because international news is so scarce, you might wish to know that news is broadcast nightly at 8pm. Hotel guests should have access to CNN and BBC World. International publications aren't available in Cuba.

PARKING   Car parking is possible in state-run *parqueos* for CUC$1–2 per night. Neighbors of casa owners will house cars in garages or provide a 24-hour street watch if the car is parked on a road for the same rate. Although your car probably won't get stolen, wipers and wheels may go walkabout. In the day, parking is easy almost anywhere because there are so few vehicles in Cuba.

PHARMACIES   Called *farmacias* in Spanish, drugstores are relatively common throughout the country, although not necessarily well stocked. Those at hospitals and major clinics are often open 24 hours. Many hotels, particularly the larger ones, have either a small pharmacy or a basic medical clinic on-site. There's a 24-hour pharmacy at the international terminal of the José Martí International Airport (☎ 7/266-4105) in Havana.

POLICE   See 'Emergency assistance', above.

SAFETY   Cuba is a relatively crime-free country, however visitors should take the usual precautions with valuables in public places and personal safety.

SENIOR TRAVELERS   Cuba is a very popular destination for older visitors. There are no discounts offered to foreign senior citizens.

SMOKING   Cuba introduced a smoking ban in enclosed public places in February 2005, but it's not really enforced. Most restaurants have non-smoking seating areas.

STAYING HEALTHY   Despite ongoing economic troubles and shortages, Cuba's healthcare system remains one of the best in Latin America. You don't need any vaccinations to travel to Cuba, unless you're coming from a region with cholera or yellow fever, in which case the Cuban authorities require proof of immunization.

Staying healthy on a trip to Cuba is predominantly a matter of common sense: Know your physical limits and don't overexert yourself in the ocean, on hikes, or in athletic activities. Cuba is a tropical country, and so limit your exposure to the sun, especially during the first few days of your trip and, thereafter, from 11am to 3pm. (It's often much hotter in Cuba between 2pm and 3pm than at midday.) Use a sunscreen with a high protection factor and apply it liberally. To avoid heat exhaustion drink plenty of water to replace lost fluids, and travel with salt replacement powders so you can rehydrate quickly if necessary. Rehydration treatment is also essential if you suffer from an upset stomach and diarrhea, another common health concern for visitors to hot countries.

In terms of biting bugs, your standard array of bees, wasps, mosquitoes, and sand fleas are present. Sand fleas are a slight nuisance at most beaches if there's no offshore breeze to clear them, particularly around sunrise and sunset. Bring repellent and wear light, long-sleeved clothing.

TAX   There's a CUC$25 departure tax payable in cash at a designated airport desk prior to the immigration checkpoint, there is an ATM in the airport.

TELEPHONES   Public phones are located all around Cuba, many of them card operated. Cards can be bought at Etecsa offices. Unfortunately, many payphones don't work.

Directory enquiries are on ☎ 113. For international operator and collect calls, call ☎ 180.

Cuba's international dialing code is ☎ 0053.

TIME Havana is 5 hours behind Greenwich Mean Time (GMT), or on a par with Eastern Standard Time (EST) in the United States and Canada. Daylight saving time is observed by setting clocks ahead 1 hour from one Sunday in March to one Sunday in October.

TIPPING Tip porters between CUC\$0.50 and CUC\$1. Some restaurants include a 10% service charge, although you should tip the waiting staff an additional 5% to 10%, depending upon the quality of service, as they don't see any of the service charge. You should tip the hotel cleaning staff around CUC\$1 a day in a hotel, and also tip the waiters who serve you every day in the all-inclusive resorts, because they earn miserable salaries.

TOURIST INFORMATION OFFICES José Martí International Airport, Arrivals Hall, ☎ 7/642-6101; open daily 10am–9pm. Calle Obispo esq Bernazas, ☎ 7/866-3333; open 9am–5pm Mon–Sat. The **Infotur** website is www.infotur.cu.

TRAVELERS WITH DISABILITIES Overall, Cuba isn't an easy country for those with disabilities. Although a few hotels are equipped for travelers with disabilities, these are far from the norm. Moreover, there's almost no private or public transportation service geared toward such travelers. The streets of Havana are rugged and crowded, and sidewalks in particular are often either totally absent or badly torn up. The Cuban people, however, are quite conscientious and embracing in their treatment of people with disabilities.

WATER Stick to bottled water, just to err on the safe side. Ask for 'agua mineral natural' (still) or 'agua mineral con gas' (sparkling water).

Cuba: **A Brief History**

Pre-Columbian History & the Spanish Conquest

1000 BC Native American tribes—the Siboney, Taíno, and Guanajatabey—numbered about 100,000 and had lived on the island since at least 1000 BC. Hunters, gatherers, and farmers, these native Cubans cultivated *cohiba* (tobacco), a crop upon which the island's economy would one day depend.

1511 Spaniard Don Diego Velázquez de Cuéllar sailed from neighboring Hispaniola with a band of about 300 conquistadores. Velázquez sailed to Baracoa and made that settlement the first of the original seven *villas* on the island.

1511–50 Velázquez and his fellow Spaniards extracted quick riches from the land and people, and made slaves of the native tribes. American Indian resistance led by the Taíno chief Hatuey failed after he was captured and burned at the stake by the Spanish. Thousands of Native Americans soon died from exposure to European viruses brought by the Spaniards. By the mid-1500s the native population had declined from more than 100,000 to a mere 3,000. The Spanish brought African slaves to Cuba in the first quarter of the 16th century. Sugar was being produced, but it had not yet become an important commodity.

Life as a Colony

1555–1762 French and British pirates coveted the island enough to conduct repeated raids on it; in 1555 Havana was sacked and decimated by the French pirate Jacques de Sores, and later Francis Drake and Henry Morgan followed similar tactics. The Spanish empire hastened to fortify the port cities of Havana (which became the capital in 1607) and Santiago de Cuba, for defensive purposes.

1762–1800 In 1762, British forces captured Havana, holding it for only a year before trading it back to Spain in exchange for Florida. Cuban trade expanded to countries other than Spain, notably the American colonies. After 1763 sugar-cane exports took off. Hundreds of thousands of African laborers were imported at the end of the 18th century to meet the demands of the sugar industry.

1850 By the middle of the 19th century, Cuba was producing one-third of the world's sugar. Half a million slaves—nearly half the population of Cuba—worked the plantations.

Toward Independence

1850–68 During the 19th century growing numbers of *criollos* (residents of Spanish descent who were born and raised in Cuba), particularly in El Oriente, the island's poorer eastern half, began to agitate for greater participation and autonomy. Carlos Manuel de Céspedes, a *criollo* plantation owner who had been involved in uprisings in Spain, led the call for Cuban independence on 10 October, 1868; he liberated slaves from his estate, La Demajagua.

1868–86 During the Ten Years' War (1868–78), which saw a short-lived Republic based in Bayamo and produced the first Constitution, 50,000 Cubans, including Céspedes himself, and more than 200,000 Spanish perished. Although Cuba remained a colony of Spain, the revolt precipitated the abolition of slavery on the island in 1886 and established the foundations of a national identity.

1895 Cuba's most esteemed patriot, José Martí, led the next and most important uprising against Spain, in 1895. From exile in the United States, he argued for Cuban freedom and formed the Cuban Revolutionary Party. Martí, today revered as the spiritual father of the Cuban nation, was killed during the Second War of Independence.

1898–1902 In February 1898, the *USS Maine*, hovering off the coast of Cuba in a show of protection for US interests on the island, sunk in Havana's harbor, killing the entire crew of 260. Spanish responsibility was never proved, but the United States seized upon the disaster as a pretext to declare war on Spain. The Spanish–American War lasted only a few months. The United States defeated the Spanish troops, and Spain surrendered its claim to the island by the end of the same year. A provisional military government took over until Cuba became an independent republic in 1902.

1902–1950s Until the 1950s, Cuba was riddled with political corruption and violence. Fulgencio Batista, though only a sergeant in the army, managed to dictate Cuba's internal affairs through a series of puppet presidents for nearly a decade before claiming the presidency outright in 1940. Though Batista retired in 1944, he staged a military coup and returned to power in 1952. Batista's corrupt dictatorship, supported by the United States, overlooked growing poverty across the country while Batista himself fattened his overseas bank accounts.

1953–55 A band of young rebels attacked the Moncada Barracks in Santiago de Cuba on 26 July, 1953. The effort failed miserably, and many of the rebels were killed or later captured. But the attack gave its young leader, a lawyer named Fidel Castro Ruz, the bully pulpit he needed. Jailed and tried for offenses against the nation, Castro's legendary 2-hour defense included the now-famous words, 'History will absolve me' (the title of Castro's revolutionary manifesto). Castro was imprisoned offshore on the Isla de la Juventud until May 1955, when Batista granted an amnesty to political prisoners.

1955–59 Castro fled to Mexico. The following year, along with a force of 80 guerrillas, including Ernesto 'Che' Guevara and Castro's brother Raúl, he arrived by boat in El Oriente. The rebel forces evolved into a formidable guerrilla army, largely through the assistance of peasants who were promised land reform in exchange for their support. Following two years of dramatic fighting, Castro's insurrection gained strength and legitimacy among a broad swath of the Cuban population. Batista saw the end in sight and on 1 January, 1959, he fled the country for the Dominican Republic. The combat-weary but triumphant rebels, known as the *barbudos* (the bearded ones), declared victory in Santiago de Cuba and then entered Havana a week later.

Cuba under Fidel Castro

1959–1960S The new government immediately reduced rents, instituted agrarian reform, and limited estates to 400 hectares (1,000 acres). It also expropriated utilities, factories, and private lands. Programs designed to eradicate illiteracy and provide universal healthcare and free schooling were launched. In the early years of Castro's reign, many thousands of people suspected of opposing the Revolution were imprisoned or sent to labor camps. In just three years, nearly a quarter of a million Cubans—mostly professionals and wealthy landowners—fled the country. Castro also promised elections that were never held.

1961 CIA-trained Cuban exiles launched an attempted overthrow of the Castro government. The Bay of Pigs mission was an utter fiasco and a severe black mark against the Kennedy administration. Castro later declared himself to be Marxist-Leninist.

FEB 1962 The US government launched a trade embargo against Cuba in retaliation for Cuba's state appropriations and seizures of US business assets. The trade embargo, and travel restrictions later imposed on most US citizens, continue to this day.

OCT 1962 The Soviet Union under Nikita Khrushchev installed 42 medium-range nuclear missiles in Cuba. A tense standoff ensued when Kennedy ordered a naval blockade on the island and demanded that the existing missiles be dismantled. The world waited anxiously for six days until

Khrushchev finally caved in to US demands to remove the missiles.

The Special Period

1990–MID-1990S Soviet trade and subsidies propped up Cuba's economy until the end of the 1980s. But the dismantling of the Soviet Union suddenly left Cuba in an untenable position, as supplies of food, oil, and hard currency were cut off while the US trade embargo continued. The Cuban government initiated a 'Special Period' in 1990—a euphemism for harsh new austerity measures and hardship to be borne by the large majority of Cubans.

Cuba under Raúl Castro

2006– In July 2006 Fidel Castro fell ill and withdrew from public life. His younger brother Raúl became acting president. Fidel Castro relinquished power in February 2008 and Raúl was unanimously elected as Cuba's new president by the country's National Assembly. After a flurry of intial reforms, some of which lifted restrictions on access to goods and services, there has been no alleviation of what is an increasingly growing economic and social crisis. In April 2009, US President Barack Obama relaxed restrictions on Cuban Americans visiting close relatives in Cuba. Raúl further announced to the world that he was ready to talk about 'everything' with the US, an unprecedented move. Fidel Castro immediately entered the public debate by saying that the US had 'misinterpreted' Raúl's gesture.

Survival **Spanish**

The official language in Cuba is Spanish. Many people working in the main tourist centers in hotels have some English, but it's not widely spoken and many *casas particulares* owners don't speak other European languages. Cubans speak fast and furiously. There's a very nasal and almost garbled quality to Cuban Spanish. Cubans tend to drop their final consonants, particularly the 's', and they don't roll their 'rr's strongly, converting the 'rr' into an almost 'i' sound in words like carro or perro. Cubans seldom use the formal 'usted' form, instead preferring to address almost everyone (except those much older or of particular social or political stature) as tú.

Likewise, you'll almost never hear the terms señor or señora as forms of address—Cubans prefer compañero and compañera. Cubans are also direct. They will almost always answer the phone with a curt 'Diga,' which translates roughly as a mix of 'Tell me,' 'Say what?,' and 'Speak.'

Basic Vocabulary & Phrases

ENGLISH	SPANISH	PRONUNCIATION
Good day	Buenos días	Bweh-nohss dee-ahss
How are you?	¿Cómo está?	Koh-moh ehss-tah?
Very well	Muy bien	Mwee byehn
Thank you	Gracias	Grah-syahss
You're welcome	De nada	Day nah-dah
Goodbye	Adiós	Ah-dyohss

ENGLISH	SPANISH	PRONUNCIATION
Please	Por favor	Pohr fah-vor
Yes	Sí	See
No	No	Noh
Excuse me (to get by someone)	Perdóneme	Pehr-doh-neh-meh
Excuse me (to begin a question)	Disculpe	Dees-kool-peh
Give me	Déme	Deh-meh
Where is . . . ?	¿Dónde está . . . ?	Dohn-deh ehss-tah?
the station	la estación	lah ehss-tah-seown
a hotel	un hotel	oon oh-tel
a gas station	una estación de servicio	oo-nah ehss-tah-seown deh sehr-bee-syoh
a restaurant	un restaurante	oon res-toh-rahn-teh
the toilet	el baño	el bah-nyoh
a good doctor	un buen médico	oon bwehn meh-thee-coh
the road to . . .	el camino a/hacia . . .	el cah-mee-noh ah/ah-syah
To the right	A la derecha	Ah lah deh-reh-chah
To the left	A la izquierda	Ah lah ees-kyehr-dah
Straight ahead	Derecho	Deh-reh-choh
I would like . . .	Quisiera . . .	Key-syehr-ah
to eat	comer	koh-mehr
a room	una habitación	oon-nah ah-bee-tah-seown
Do you have . . . ?	¿Tiene usted . . . ?	Tyeh-neh oos-ted?
How much is it?	¿Cuánto cuesta?	Kwahn-toh kwehss-tah?
When?	¿Cuándo?	Kwahn-doh?
What?	¿Qué?	Kay?
There is (Is there . . . ?)	(¿)Hay (. . . ?)	Eye?
What is there?	¿Qué hay?	Keh eye?
Yesterday	Ayer	Ah-yer
Today	Hoy	Oy
Tomorrow	Mañana	Mah-nyah-nah
Good	Bueno	Bweh-noh
Bad	Malo	Mah-loh
Better (best)	(Lo) Mejor	(Loh) Meh-hor
More	Más	Mahs
Less	Menos	Meh-nohss
No smoking	Se prohibe fumar	Seh pro-hee-beh foo-mahr

Numbers

1	uno	ooh-noh
2	dos	dohss
3	tres	trehss
4	cuatro	kwah-troh
5	cinco	seen-koh
6	seis	sayss

Numbers *(cont.)*

7	siete	syeh-teh
8	ocho	oh-choh
9	nueve	nweh-beh
10	diez	dyess
11	once	ohn-seh
12	doce	doh-seh
13	trece	treh-seh
14	catorce	kah-tor-seh
15	quince	keen-seh
16	dieciseis	dyess-ee-sayss
17	diecisiete	dyess-ee-syeh-teh
18	dieciocho	dyess-ee-oh-choh
19	diecinueve	dyess-ee-nweh-beh
20	veinte	bayn-teh
30	treinta	trayn-tah
40	cuarenta	kwah-ren-tah
50	cincuenta	seen-kwen-tah
60	sesenta	seh-sehn-tah
70	setenta	seh-ten-tah
80	ochenta	oh-chen-tah
90	noventa	noh-behn-tah
100	cien	syehn
200	doscientos	doh-syehn-tohs
500	quinientos	kee-nyehn-tohs
1,000	mil	meel

Days of the Week

Monday	lunes	(loo-nehss)
Tuesday	martes	(mahr-tehss)
Wednesday	miércoles	(myehr-koh-lehs)
Thursday	jueves	(wheh-behss)
Friday	viernes	(byehr-nehss)
Saturday	sábado	(sah-bah-doh)
Sunday	domingo	(doh-meen-goh)

More Useful Phrases

ENGLISH	SPANISH	PRONUNCIATION
Do you speak English?	¿Habla usted inglés?	Ah-blah oo-sted een-glehss?
Is there anyone here who speaks English?	¿Hay alguien aquí que hable inglés?	Eye ahl-gyehn ah-key keh ah-bleh een-glehss?
I speak a little Spanish.	Hablo un poco de español.	Ah-bloh oon poh-koh deh ehss-pah-nyol
I don't understand Spanish very well.	No (lo) entiendo muy bien el español.	Noh (loh) ehn-tyehn-do mwee byehn el ehss-pah-nyol
The meal is good.	Me gusta la comida.	Meh goo-stah lah koh-mee-dah
What time is it?	¿Qué hora es?	Keh oh-rah ehss?

ENGLISH	SPANISH	PRONUNCIATION
May I see your menu?	¿Puedo ver el menú (la carta)?	Pweh-doh vehr el meh-noo (lah car-tah)?
The check, please.	La cuenta, por favor.	Lah kwehn-tah, pohr fah-vor
What do I owe you?	¿Cuánto le debo?	Kwahn-toh leh deh-boh?
What did you say?	¿Cómo? (colloquial expression for American 'Eh?')	Koh-moh?
I want (to see) . . .	Quiero (ver) . . .	Kyehr-oh (vehr)
a room	un cuarto or una habitación	oon kwar-toh, oon-nah ah-bee-tah-seown
for two persons	para dos personas	pah-rah dohss pehr-soh-nahs
with (without) bathroom	con (sin) baño	kohn (seenbah-nyoh
We are staying here only . . .	Nos quedamos aquí solamente . . .	Nohs keh-dahm-ohss ah-key sohl-ah-mehn-teh
one night	una noche	oon-ah noh-cheh
one week	una semana	oon-ah seh-mahn-ah
We are leaving . . .	Partimos (Salimos) . . .	Pahr-tee-mohss (sah-lee-mohss)
tomorrow	mañana	mah-nya-nah
Do you accept . . . ?	¿Acepta usted . . . ?	Ah-sehp-tah oo-sted?
traveler's checks?	cheques de viajero?	cheh-kehs deh byah-heh-ro?
credit cards?	tarjeta de crédito?	tar-hay-ta de kray-dee-toe?

Cuban **Cuisine**

Local Eating
Cuban, or *criolla,* cuisine is a mix of European (predominantly Spanish) and Afro-Caribbean influences. The staples include roasted and fried pork, beef, and chicken, usually accompanied by rice, beans, plantains, and yucca. Oddly, Cubans don't eat large amounts of seafood, although fish and lobster dishes are on the menu at most tourist restaurants. In general, Cuban cuisine doesn't use aggressive amounts of spice or hot peppers, although onions, garlic, and, to a much lesser extent, cumin are used fairly liberally.

Meals are accompanied by some combination of white rice and beans. *Arroz moro,* or *moros y cristianos* (Moors and Christians), is the common name for black beans mixed with white rice. *Congrí* is a similar dish of red beans and white rice already mixed. The national dish—which, unfortunately, you won't often find on restaurant menus, but is worth sampling if you do—is *ajiaco,* a chunky meat and vegetable stew. *Ajiaco* comes from the Taino word *aji* for chile pepper, although the dish is seldom prepared very spicy.